PLACE N

AROUND

GRANTOWN-ON-SPEY

Place Names of the Parish of Cromdale, Inverallan & Advie

By C.J.Halliday MA(Hons). MSc. BDS. FSA(Scot)

Published by C J Halliday

Publishing partner: Paragon Publishing, Rothersthorpe
First published 2018
© C J Halliday 2018

ISBN 978-1-78222-553-9

Book design, layout and production management by Into Print
www.intoprint.net
+44 (0)1604 832149

Printed and bound in UK and USA by Lightning Source

Dedicated to the many local folk who helped me and wanted their place names to be remembered. Especially: Bill Campbell, George Dixon, Bill Sadler, Graeme Stuart, the late Madge McQueen and the late Professor Bill Nicholaisen for his encouragement.

And Peter Mackintosh 1876-1967, Connie Mackintosh 1915-2005, Chrissie Mackintosh 1917-2001,
John Mackintosh 1920-1991 and Betty Mackintosh 1925-2017 of Achosnich.

To the people and place names
Let them not be forgotten

Achosnich Cottage, Grantown-on-Spey PH26 3PR, Scotland, UK
christopherjohnhalliday@gmail.com

Contents

Acknowledgements

Acknowledgements are due to many individuals and organisations. Thanks go to the archivists and staff at the Historical Search Room of the National Records of Scotland and the map department of the National Records of Scotland in Thomas Thomson House, Edinburgh. Reproductions from Timothy Pont, Strathspey, 1583-96 and The Military Survey of Scotland, 1747-1755 are by kind permission of The National Library of Scotland and Historic Environment Scotland. Also to the Seafield Estate for permission to use material from their extensive record and map collection GD248 in the National Records of Scotland. Gwen Walker for her sketches and artistry from my scribbles. Finally members of the Grantown Society for their local knowledge and encouragement to see this through to completion.

Welcome to Grantown-on-Spey

Preface

I was four months old when I first visited my Highland relations near Grantown. It was the first of many holidays spent out on the hill herding sheep and cattle or as a teenager out on the moor, grouse beating with some colourful local characters. But above all was the freedom, the freedom to explore the hills and abandoned farms from a bygone age.

My bonds with the area are strong on both my paternal and maternal lines. Three of my grandparents were born in the parish and two of my great grandfathers; William McGregor of Camerory and William Mackintosh of Achosnich, contributed to the Ordinance Survey Name Books for the parish in 1868. Both were Gaelic speakers. My McGregor line lived in the vicinity of Castle Grant since at least 1680 and the Mackintoshes in the 1780s were at Torspardon near Skye of Curr. They never moved far for marriage, so the connections run deep with numerous local families and places.

Walking the hills I was always curious. What's the name of a ruin, what did it mean and who had once lived there? Often this could simply be answered by asking a local. Sadly over the years, I've seen the native rural population decline and with it the precious local knowledge, that can't be found in any book or on the internet. Oh how I wish I'd asked even more questions from those who were the sole repositories of local lore.

Gathering notes over the years and after many false starts, I began not only working at a desk, pouring over the wonderful Seafield collection of estate maps, but also field work; walking the parish from the Beum a'Chlaidheimh to Tulchan and Lochindorb to Tullochgorm and the Cromdale Hills. I visited and photographed the majority of places listed, 'bagging' them like they were Munros. Some areas I thought I knew like the back of my hand, yet the detailed 18th century maps by Taylor and later Brown revealed a world I had barely discovered. It was fun and challenging to do. Few I think will have covered so much of the parish on foot. I hope the following goes some way in recording and preserving the place names and language of the people of Cromdale, Inverallan and Advie parish.

Any errors or omissions are entirely mine. I would be pleased to know if readers see any errors, or know any names that are not listed.

The Parish

The parish of Cromdale, Inverallan and Advie now solely exists as an ecclesiastical district within the Presbytery of Abernethy. From 1845 civil parishes for local government administration were also established and existed until 1930, broadly covering the same geographic area as the ecclesiastical parishes. However the land and boundary changes for this parish are not simple. Subjected to various parish and county boundary changes over the years, its extent ranged from about 16 miles long and 12 miles broad. It was bounded in the east by Inveravon and Knockando, on the west by Abernethy and Duthil, on the south by Kirkmichael and on the north by parts of Edinkillie and Ardclach.

Initially three distinct separate parishes of Cromdale, Inverallan and Advie, the first amalgamaton was in 1593 between Advie and Cromdale followed in 1618 with Inverallan. Land ownership was also in a constant state of flux with the expansive plans of the Lairds of Clan Grant ebbing and flowing over the centuries. The Laird of Grant was the sole proprietor of the whole parish and his estate provided much of the employment and accommodation for the parishioners, whose lives were linked inexorably to the rise and fall of the prosperity of the family of Grant.

The majority of the population which on average amounted to 3000 lived in the southern quarter of the parish, along the River Spey, and also the area between Castle Grant and the River Spey and it was in this area that most of the agriculture of the parish was undertaken. Numerous agricultural improvements and the founding of the new town of Grantown in 1765, benefited the people who were able to take advantage of these developments. However the changes in agriculture meant that many fewer workers were needed on the lands and many were forced to leave the parish for the central belt of Scotland or seek their fortune overseas.

Central and local government radically altered the historic parish and county boundaries, so the parish and Grantown, 'The Captial of Strathspey' often felt in no mans land between Inverness-shire and Moray, Highland Region and Grampian Region and currently Highland and Moray Councils.

A time line of dates and land transactions, will hopefully simplify key events

- Between the years 1223 and 1242, Walter de Moravia granted the deed of Inverallan to Andrew, Bishop of Moray for upholding the cathedral of Elgin.

- 1226 Cromdale in hands of the Earl of Fife.

- 1288 Robert de Augustus, Lord of Inverallan.

- 1316 John le Grant holds lands of Inverallan.

- 1357 Lands of Inverallan consist of 3 davochs: Kildreke 1 davoch, Glenbeg ½, Craggan 1 and Gaich ½ davoch.

- 1379 Curr, Clurie and Tullochgorm held by Sir Alexander Stuart, Lord of Badenoch and later the Earl of Huntly. Formed part of the Lordship of Badenoch.

- 1431 Nairn family hold Lethindie, castle, mill, Achroisk, Kirktown of Cromdale, Delachaple and Rinaballoch.

- 1489 Barony of Freuchie held by Sir Duncan Grant of Freuchie and Balachastell (the town of the castle).

- 1491 John Grant of Freuchie purchases Tullochgorm, Curr and Clurie from Earl of Huntly.

- 1493 John Grant as chief now styled himself as 'of Freuchie' after the current location of Castle Grant and annexed the lands of Fruquie, two Culfoichs, Dalfour, Downan, Auchingall, and Auchnarrows and was granted a charter from James IV, raising these lands to the Barony of Freuchie.

- 1553 The castle known as Freuchie was restyled to the Castle and Fortalice of Ballachastell.

- 1586 The two Achnarrows, Dunan and Port purchased by John Grant of Freuchie.

- 1587 the lands of Inverallan, Glenbeg, Gaich, Craggan and Dreggie were sold to John Grant of Freuchie for 6000 merks. These lands though formerly the property of the Grants, had passed for a time out of their hands after a series of disputes.

- 1592 James VI confirmed a charter for the adjacent lands of Auchnarrows, Downan and Port and together with those of Inverallan were shortly afterwards included in the new Barony of Cromdale.

- 1593 Advie parish annexed to Cromdale Parish.

- 1600 John Grant of Freuchy exchanged with the Earl of Huntly the lands of Glenlivet and Strathaven for Curr, Clury and Tullochgorum in Inverallan, which were part of the sixteen davochs of the Lordship of Badenoch and to which the Loch and Castle of Lochindorb also belonged.

- 1609 John Grant, 5th Laird of Freuchie acquired the lands of Cromdale from Thomas Nairn and along with those lands of Inverallan and others obtained from the Crown an erection into the Burgh of Barony of Cromdale.

- 1611 A rental of the Barony of Inverallan, describes the levy due for 'Glenbeg, Gaeycht, Cragan and Dregie with the milns and fischings thairof '.

- 1618 Inverallan and Cromdale parishes united.

- A Charter of 1694 to Ludovick Grant, 8th of Freuchie by King William and Queen Mary ordained that, 'the town formerly called Casteltown of Freuquie, now and in all time to come to be called the Town and Burgh of Grant, and to be the principal burgh of regality, a market cross to be erected therein and proclamations to be made thereat.'

- From that time forth, he became known as Ludovick Grant of Grant and his residence called Castle Grant.

- From 1845 until 1930, civil parishes formed part of Scotland's local government system. The parishes originally had their origins in the ecclesiastical parishes of the Established Church of Scotland. Often overlapped the then existing county boundaries, largely because they reflected earlier territorial divisions.

- In 1869 a Quoad Sacra parish of Inverallan was established within the parish, principally to serve the growing population in Grantown and former parish of Inverallan.

- 1870 The Inverness and Elgin County Boundaries Act, saw part of the united parishes of Cromdale and Inverallan, including Grantown, transferred from Inverness-shire to Moray.

- 1889 Local Government (Scotland) Act saw further changes. The county boundaries remained the same but the Inverness-shire part of the parish was transferred to the Inverness-shire parish of Duthil and Rothiemurchus. This stretched from Clachbain and Auchnahannet to Muckerach, Clury and Tullochgorm.

- 1898 Grantown became a Police Burgh and the name changed to Grantown-on-Spey.

- 1930 saw the demise of the parish as a civil area of administration in Scotland. They were grouped into elected district councils.

- 1975 Following the Local Government (Scotland) Act 1973, the district councils were abolished and new local authorities established that often cut across civil parish boundaries. Grantown and Cromdale at a stroke severed their long historical connections with Moray and became part of the District of Badenoch & Strathspey within Highland Region. Administered from Kingussie and Inverness.

- 1996 Further re-organisation of Scotland followed the Local Government (Scotland) Act 1994 which saw the demise of the Regions and Districts and the formation of the Highland Council Area.

- The three current Community Council areas of Grantown, Cromdale & Advie and Dulnain Bridge closely follow the historical boundaries of the former parish.

- 2003 The Cairngorms National Park, the second largest National Park in Scotland was created. It was further extended in 2010 to include parts of Highland Perthshire and Glenshee. However a large area in the north of the former parish, around Dava and Lochindorb, and in the east around Tulchan and Advie were not included in the National Park. Old historical county and parish boundaries which followed natural topography were ignored.

The Cairngorms National Park

Mapping the Parish

Before the Ordnance Survey first surveyed this area in the late 1860's, the best available maps and plans were those commissioned by the the lairds of Grant and Earls of Seafield. There are two earlier maps by Timothy Pont and William Roy, from the 16th and 18th centuries which have greatly contributed to our understanding of Cromdale and Inverallan and both are invaluable recordings of place names and their locations from a bygone age.

Pont, Strath Spey ca.1583-1596
©The National Library of Scotland

Timothy Pont

Timothy Pont was born about 1565 in Fife, the son of a prominent cleric. After studying at St Andrews University from 1580-1583, he appears to have spent the late 1580s and the 1590s travelling throughout Scotland, mapping the country. When the Dutch cartographer Blaeu compiled his atlas in 1654, thirty six maps of Scotland were attributed to the work of Pont. Scotland was then the best mapped country in the world. Between 1601 and 1610 Pont was the minister of Dunnet in Caithness and is believed to have died by 1614.

His maps provide invaluable information about Scottish place names. They are the earliest cartographic and also the earliest source of any kind, textual or graphic. His ability to record names as he heard them provides valuable clues to the late 16th century pronunciation of names. Pont's place name information was not surpassed until the Roy Military Survey and county maps of the 18th century.

His map of Strathspey done at some point between1583-1596 covered 'Kromdell Parish, Innerellan and Skiravy' and recorded many places still recognisable today: Freuchy, Achnarrabeg, Poirt, Achroskie, Glentuilchen, Knockenbuy and Shenvall. His maps were relatively accurate sketches from life and give an idea of the appearance of many buildings that have subsequently altered or disappeared. Among them sketches of both Castle Grant (Ballachastal) and Lethendry castle are the earliest visual records for both buildings.

Pont also made notes on his maps with points of interest. He mentioned at the head of Glen Tulchan a long forgotten encounter; 'At Badinlochan, a skirmish by the Grants against the clan Chattan (McIntosh)'.

William Roy

The Military Survey of Scotland, 1747-1755 was undertaken after the Jacobite rising of 1745. It was the first systematic mapping of the Scottish mainland. In 1756 Lt Col Watson, the Deputy Quartermaster General of North Britain, had talks with the Duke of Cumberland, and a plan for the detailed and accurate mapping of the Highlands was drawn up. The resulting survey has become so closely identified with its chief surveyor, William Roy (1726-1790), that it is often called The Roy Map. There was only one surveying party under Roy, which started in 1747 in the Fort Augustus area, but after two years five more parties were involved. Each team consisted of: a surveyor, an NCO and six soldiers.

Only selected landscape features such roads, rivers and lochs were surveyed with instruments. Towns, settlements and hills were sketched in by eye or copied from other maps. This lead to some quite wide variations in recording villages and farms, with many missing. Place names are often quite variable, sometimes reflecting local pronunciation and recorded by surveyors who were unfamiliar with Gaelic and Scots language.

Roy described his maps as a 'magnificent military sketch, than a very accurate map of the country'. Yet his maps of Strathspey provide a unique record of an overwhelmingly rural society in which a runrig, unenclosed system of agriculture was still the norm and of a landscape largely unaffected as yet by the enormous changes caused by the agricultural revolution of the late 18th century onwards.

One hundred and twenty two place names in the parish appear on Roy's map, some of which have subsequently disappeared, either from modern maps or everyday usage. It's also surprising the names of familiar locations known today, often don't appear. The most visually striking difference is the absence of Grantown-on-Spey as we know it. The current town was not founded for another fourteen years after Roy's map was completed. However the military road and Old Spey Bridge across the River Spey are present, and became key factors in deciding the setting for the current town.

Roy depicted settlements and buildings with red dots, agricultural land with hatching and cleverly achieved the sense of gradient and direction of slope for hills with creative shading. The visual impact conveys the topography of the landscape without the presence of contour lines or a recognised scale. Although not an accurate representation as to numbers and acreage, it does however show where such activities were active in the mid 18th century within the parish.

Alexander and George Taylor

Many of the first maps and plans within the Seafield Papers are attributed to Alexander (c.1746-1828) and George Taylor, both of whom became eminent land surveyors. The first reference to them appears on 3 Nov 1766. It's possible that the Taylor brothers were the sons of William Taylor, surveyor at Fort George, who was working in the northeast from 1756-1766. His sudden disappearance from the records in 1766 and a reference in 1767 to survey James Grant of Grant's estates on Speyside, that 'the surveyor has a couple of lads who are bred to this business and can measure land by themselves' lead to this conclusion. On recommendation, Alexander Taylor applied to Grant of Grant early in 1768 to engage as a salaried surveyor. One of his first tasks that year was to make 'A plan of New Grantown with the lands of Kylentra, Easter and Wester Dreggy, etc'. In 1770 he moved on to work for the Duke of Gordon for a salary of £35 per annum and his place with Grant of Grant was taken by brother, George. George completed the survey of Speyside and Abernethy which was bound into a volume of thirty two splendid plans.

At the turn of the 19th century George Brown (1747-1816) continued surveying many areas and his detailed maps are a rich source of field names for small and large farms on the estate.

Ordnance Survey

The Ordnance Survey Act 1841 was followed in 1843 with the start of the six inch to one mile survey, but it was not until 1866 that surveying began in Inverness-shire and Moray. The parish appears to have been surveyed between 1868 and 1871. Ledgers called the 'Original Object Name Books' were also kept to record the names of local places and features with notes of historical interest. However the people supplying the information to the recorder were not always those most qualified to do so and the authorities had the final say on what became the final name on the map. The Survey's remit was to contact the 'best authorities' and to do so mindful of locals' social standing: owners before others, 'respectable inhabitants' at all times before persons, such as small farmers and cottagers, who were 'not to be depended on, even for the names of the places they occupy'.

The system was frought with potential problems for the spoken word, especially in a Gaelic speaking, possibly illiterate population, not being the word that finally appeared on the map. Examination of the 'Original Object Name Books' or Ordnance Survey Name Books [OSNB] does show different spellings for a place, but one version then became the 'official' recognised one. Differences can be seen between placenames used by officialdom and those in common usage on farm signs, correspondence within families, gravestones and in family bibles.

Roy's Military Map 1747-1755, Inverallan ©The British Library

The Gaelic Influence

Gaelic had by far the greatest influence on place names within the parish, almost to the total exclusion of English, with the exception in the new town of Grantown founded in 1765. The number of Gaelic and Gaelic and English speakers were enumerated in the 1891 census. The results show the last strongholds of the language were the areas of Achnahannet (Dulnain), Tulchan, Cromdale and Dava. There were only three monoglot Gaelic speakers left by 1891 and of those only one was a native of the parish. Janet Grant aged 84 and deaf, who lived with her sister at Craigdhu near the Braes of Castle Grant, was very likely the last locally born resident to have had no English.

Though spoken into the 20th century, its decline had been noted a hundred years before, with the gradual ingress of Scots/English. In 1792-93 the Rev Lewis Grant, minister at Cromdale in the First or Old Statistical Account wrote:

'The common people speak the Gaelic tongue, but the English is the prevailing language, which they pronounce with great propriety and with very little of the brogue. In all the parishes southwards from this English alone is spoken, but here both languages are preached daily. In a few years hence, the English will be the only language as the people send their children to read the scriptures and for this purpose often in the winter 4 or 5 schools are employed at one in the parish at their own expense'.

And in the later Second Statistical Account of 1841 the Rev James Grant also of Cromdale wrote:

'Gaelic is the language generally spoken by the great body of the common people, particularly the old, but almost the whole population young and old speak and understand the English language. Indeed in the lower part of the parish English is preferred, due to its proximity to Inveravon and Knockando where no Gaelic is spoken'.

However schools were to have a profound effect accelerating the decline in the language. Prior to the 1872 Education (Scotland Act), some schools under the Scottish Society for Promoting Christian Knowledge (SSPCK) did use Gaelic as the medium of teaching, but their prime objective was to use the scriptures to promote the use of English.

The introduction of the1872 Act, effectively put an end to

non-English medium education and led to the discouragement of Gaelic, with pupils being punished by teachers for speaking the language. Pressure upon the Scottish Education Department in the years immediately following the Act saw the gradual reintroduction of certain measures providing for the use of Gaelic in schools. This pressure led to the undertaking by the department of a survey in 1876 which revealed a "distinct majority" of school boards within the Highlands in favour of the inclusion of Gaelic within the curriculum, although it also revealed that some of those in Gaelic-speaking areas were against this. None of the school boards in Strathspey wished Gaelic taught in their schools.

The repercussions didn't take long to show, even in those areas where the language had been at its healthiest. The HM Inspector's Report has an entry in the Dava School Log Book dated 7 Jan 1878:

'The school is situated in a Gaelic speaking district and is taught by an English speaking teacher, but the difficulties of the situation whether real or imagined are very well overcome'.

Miss Coventry, the teacher in question, was a native of Clackmannanshire. An account survives of the changes that affected communication across the generations.

Charles Grant a retired shoemaker in Grantown was interviewed about his life in 1907. He was born in 1829, the year of the famous Moray Floods and aged around ten went off to Angus for work. It didn't take long for him to learn to speak the dialect of the county and when he returned after about 18 months absence, meeting his grandfather, who always spoke Gaelic, could not understand a word of broad Scots, while the grandfather's language was a mystery to Charles.

From the 1891 census it's possible to break down the parish by Gaelic speakers into approximately the areas that are covered by the following chapters, excluding Grantown.

Auchnahannet, Dulnain, Skye of Curr to Tullochgorm
100 households with a population of 437 of whom 57% spoke Gaelic.

Ballintomb, Gaich, Gorton, Lynmacgregor, Ballieward:
50 households with a population of 248 of whom 38% spoke Gaelic

Castle Grant, The Braes, Delliefure
51 households with a population of 249 of whom 52% spoke Gaelic

Tulchan
41 households with a population of 181 of whom 32% spoke Gaelic
Dava
90 households with a population of 382 of whom 48% spoke Gaelic
Cromdale and Advie
131 households with a population of 508 of whom 24% spoke Gaelic

These revealing figures show a marked decline of Gaelic speakers from the west and north of the parish to the east and south. There was a clear demarcation along the parish boundary with the neighbouring parishes in Moray and Banff, where English or Scots were the prevailing means of communication. Also within the population those able to speak Gaelic were dominated by above 45 years of age and in the eastern area by those over 60. It was clear that the language was already in marked decline with the younger generation.

One would have expected the Dava with 48% to have at least matched or bettered the Braes on 52%, both more remote with similar social and economic groups. However the coming of the railway in 1863 had seen an influx of railway surfacemen and station staff, come from areas that were not Gaelic speaking.

Eddie Calder a native of Dava, in the early 1990s speaking of his childhood said he had no Gaelic, but both his parents spoke it, though only to each other on subjects they didn't want the children to hear. No children in his day spoke it and he only knew a few words, and not very good ones!

So in less than a hundred years the Strathspey Gaelic dialect had become extinct. Radio, TV and greater mobility for work had also accelerated the process. Only the place names the people gave to their landscape, are left as testament to their rich culture, history and way of life.

The Land of Hills and Moors

Walking in and around Grantown one is constantly aware of the views to the hills on all sides, and place names aptly categorise them by height, size, shape, colour and texture. There's an old misleading cliché that the Inuit have several words to describe snow, and similarly here, a hill is not just a hill.

There is only one *ben* in the parish, Beinn Mhor, which usually denotes the highest elevation in an area, but at 471m or 1545ft, it is lower than many others both near and far. Perhaps as it stands unconnected on three sides to adjoining hills, sets it apart and the views from the top are worthy of its name.

Carn, literally heap of stones is more widespread especially in the Dava and Tulchan. Usually qualified by colour or descriptive location: Geal Charn (white hill), Carn Ruigh an Uain (hill of the lamb shieling).

Cnoc or *Knock* are small hillocks or mounds, to be found on lower land, often in isolation. In the Allt Breac valley, two in particular stand out: Knockannaceardich (hillock of the smith) and Knockannakeist (hillock of the chest or coffin), while near Castle Grant, Cnoc Freuchie (heathery hillock) or more commonly called Freuchie Hillock, an ancient site of some significance with the discovery of a Pictish Class 1 stone .

Sgorr appears just twice; in Glen Tulchan and on the watershed track to the Ourack. In both cases called Sgor Gaoithe, peak of the wind, the latter with commanding views over Strathspey and the Cairngorms to the south and north over the Moray Firth, Black Isle and beyond.

Sithean or fairy hills are frequently found especially in Glen Tulchan and Dava. To the trained eye they can sometimes be picked out in the landscape, looking like inverted Christmas puddings. The *Sithean* south of Drumroy no longer qualifies for inclusion on modern maps, but its significance in the locality is evident with the number of associated place names: Allt Loch an t-Sidhein, Loch an t-Sidhein, Ryndian.

Sron a nose or promontory are projections from the main bulk of a hill. Across the ravine from Huntly's Cave is Sron na Grandach where an unfortunate individual standing in an exposed position was allegedly shot with an arrow by cattle thieves. Sron na

Saobhaidhe in Glen Tulchan was frequented by foxes or the profile of the hillside looks like a fox's snout.

Tom, usually a small round hillock or knoll is particularly common in Cromdale. Tom an Uird, Tom na Coinnich, Tom a' Cait, Tom Lethendry.

Torr can vary from an isolated rock to rising high ground. Torrispardon near Clurie is the hill of the hen roost, describing the level intermittent shelves on the hillside, rather than literally a hen roost. And Tormore (large hill) which is now a famous distillery.

Gleann or glen occurs only on the northern side of the parish, where longer burns rising in the hills gradually muster in size and gather speed onwards to the River Spey. Glen Beag (little valley), Glen Tulchan (valley of little hillocks) and Glen Gheallaidh (shining valley)

Clash, Lag and Glac, all describe declivities and all are numerous in the parish. Though it's difficult to distinguish if any, the differences implied by size, depth or steepness. *Clash* is more a small ravine or sudden fissure in the land, best seen at Clais an Dunain . This hidden picturesque gulley has steeply wooded sides and a strong defensive position, ideally chosen for the small motte of Grant's Fort. Likewise Clais Mhor (large hollow) and Clais Gharbh (rough hollow) are obvious narrow defiles in the landscape. Ballinlagg (farmstead of the hollow), Laggan (little hollow), and Lag nan Caorach (hollow of the sheep) are examples of *Lag*, a more shallow natural depression. *Glac* is somewhere in between, Glac na Saobhaidh (hollow of the fox).

Tir, the word for land surprisingly rarely features except out by Lochindorb, where on the south side opposite the castle is Tiriebeg (little land) and on the opposing northerly shore in the parish of Edinkillie, its more famous literary counterpart from 'The Key Above the Door', Tiriemore (large land).

Blaar is an open space of moorland, of which several are to be found on the Dava moor. They're usually descriptive of an adjoining human habitation, Blaar Druimruigh (moss of the red ridge), Blaar Glengour (moss of the goats) and Blaar Ryluachrach (moss of the rushes shieling). *Blaar* although a boggy wet area, seems to refer more to an area that was suitable for cutting peat, than noting it was a bog. Thus the association with the name of a property identified each farms peat moss for fuel.

Srath of course applies to Strathspey, the flat riverside land adjoining the River Spey and traditionally was the area between the two Craigellachies, homeland of Clan Grant. *Haugh*, a Scots word likewise is a term to describe flat alluvial land beside a river on the floor of a valley, notably the Haughs of Cromdale.

Torspardon

The Land of Lochs, Rivers and Burns

Lochs are few in number in the parish, confined to the north side of the Spey, though what is lacking in quantity is made up for in quality and mystique. Lochindorb is a beautiful, if unpredictable stretch of water, famed for the ruined castle on its island setting. Home to the Wolf of Badenoch it witnessed many historical events before its demise. Water kelpies were also known to frequent its waters and those of nearby Lochan Eilein (island loch), famed for its floating island, known to move mysteriously across the water surface assisted by witches.

Allt or burns are numerous in Cromdale and Tulchan, their short, direct courses, draining the steeper hillsides to the rivers below. They're often descriptive of an adjoining feature: Allt na Loine Mhoir (burn of the large marsh), Allt Luchair (burn of the rushes), Allt Creag an Tarmachan (burn of the ptarmigan rock) and the lovely Allt Suileagach (burn of eyes), to describe the bubbles created in the churning water.

Caochan also a burn or stream, appears to be one of lesser volume or ferocity. They tend to have simple identifying names, often colours. There are numerous Caochan Ruadh (red burn) and Caochan Dubh (black or dark burn) and Caochan Ban (white burn). They could just be points of reference but the colours do sometimes describe the features of the burns. Red the colour of the pebbles on the water bed, black or dark the peaty water or a shady location and white, the colour of the surrounding vegetation. There are many Gaelic words for grades of colour and shade. They describe more muted natural colours found in nature, rather than pillar box red and snow white.

Feith, a vein or sinew, appropriately describes the numerous, narrow, slowly flowing water channels in a bog: Feith a'Chaoruinn (bog stream of the rowan tree) and Feith a'Mhor Fhir (morass of the large man).

All these sources of water arise from somewhere and two words are used for a spring or well. *Fuaran* and *tobar*. The latter sometimes used for a man made well, but appears to be interchangeable with fuaran here. Fuaran More (large spring), Tobar Alain (well of the green place).

And of course *Inbhir*, a familiar place name in Scotland for the mouth of a river or burn, gives our parish of Inverallan its name. Where the Allan, Glen Beg or Craggan Burn, take your pick, as they're all names for the same stretch of water, finally enters the Spey beside old Inverallan cemetery. Interestingly it retains the original old name at the source and confluence, yet changes identity on route.

Inverallan

Flora and Fauna

The most prevalent tree name in the parish is *beith*, the birch, which appears with: hills, Creag Bheithe Bheag (little birch rock), burns, Allt Clais Bheithe (burn of the birch hollow) and farms, Dalvey (birch meadow). Any reference to Scots pine *giuthas*, appears to be for solitary trees or isolated clumps, Drumuish (pine ridge) and Creag a' Ghiubhais (rock of the pine),rather than the large plantations started by the Lairds of Grant. Other less commonly named trees and shrubs are the rowan *caorann*, Feith a' Chaoruinn (bog of the rowan tree), gorse *aitean*, Carn Aighteen Du (hill of the black gorse), broom *bealaidh,* Cnocan-a-Bealaidh (broom hillock) and of course the ubiquitous heather, *fraoch* Freuchie (heathery place) and Rynruich (heather shieling).

Mammals are identified usually by places of habitation, so rock of the cat, den of the fox and place of the pig. There is also Loch Mhadadh, loch of the wolf, which perhaps gives a connection to a past inhabitant, extinct since the 18th century. Horses and sheep are frequently mentioned too, especially in those areas associated with summer shielings and grazing.

Birds in the generic unspecified species *nan euan* are used for Caochan nan Eun (stream of the birds) both for a stream and a croft of the same name. Commonly used in local place names are raptors, the eagle, Creag na h-Iolaire (rock of the eagle), and buzzard, Buinne nan Clamhan (stream or torrent of the buzzards on the Spey) Opposite Huntly's Cave, the rocky cliff face was once the haunt of the raven, Creag an Fhithich and the burn below, the Allt an Fhithich. Seagulls are known to nest by the secluded hill lochans and Lochan na Stuirteag (loch of the blackheaded gull) was once a well- known source of gulls eggs.

In Cromdale there is Balnafettack (homestead of the plover) and Creag an Tarmachain (the ptarmigan rock), a bird still seen in its winter plumage on the Cromdale Hills.

Settlement

Baile or Bal is the most commonly used Gaelic word for a permanent settlement, so naturally found on good agricultural land. It's usually now the name of farms along the low lying land beside the River Spey and less frequently at a higher altitude, where the land is less fertile and conditions less favourable for crops. Ballintomb, Balvattan, Balnacruie, Balmenach and Balnafettack are all examples that survive today. These larger farms also had names for their fields, which are often descriptive of their location, type of soil, crop and productivity. The early estate maps from the late 18th century are perhaps the only surviving record of these names, as they've fallen out of use or fields have been merged.

Achadh was first used as the prefix for a field name, but later was used as the name of a permanent settlement: Achnafearn (field of the alder), Achosnich (field of sighing) and Auchnahannet (field of the church or chapel). There are two Auchnahannets, nestling within remote areas of the parish. Both are of great antiquity and were once on old routes from Strathspey to Lochindorb and the low lands of Moray. Field names from the old maps help identify their positions, though nothing remains of the former structures nor any record of their history.

Davochs appear in many of the old estate rentals for the parish. Though considered a measure of land, probably as far back as the Pictish period, there is still confusion as to their true extent. Some consider it was the amount of land that could be tilled by eight oxen or just the acreage of pasture covering about 416 acres. However in reality there appears no set quantity of land, with great variations from one davoch to another. They do however provide neat divisions of the parish, that varied little over the centuries and appear not only in the estate correspondence, but on the 18th century estate maps and plans. Often they are neatly marked out, listing the properties within each davoch, including in some cases the tenants' names.

Ruighe is the slope of a hillside or in Strathspey can also be a shieling. The Dava moor has several: Rynechra, Rychorrach, Ryluachrach, Ryndian, Rychraggan and Rynuan. Place names for sheep, horses, goats and even butter (Tom Ime, butter hillock)) are often found in the same vicinity. A strong indication of the transhumance activity that previously took place. The 18th century agricultural improvements in many cases, led to these seasonal summer residences becoming permanent settlements.

Allt Dearg

Lyntaurie

Lethendry Castle

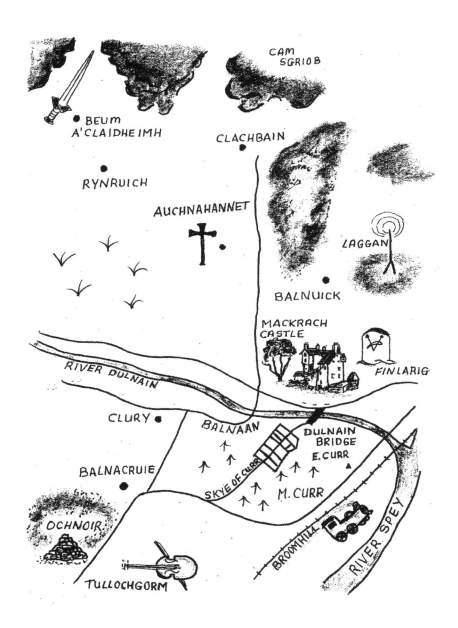

CAM SGRIOB

BEUM A'CLAIDHEIMH

CLACHBAIN

RYNRUICH

AUCHNAHANNET

LAGGAN

BALNUICK

MACKRACH CASTLE

FINLARIG

RIVER DULNAIN

CLURY

BALNAAN

DULNAIN BRIDGE
E. CURR

BALNACRUIE

SKYE OF CURR

M. CURR

OCHNOIR

BROOMHILL

RIVER SPEY

TULLOCHGORM

CHAPTER 1

Auchnahannet, Dulnain Bridge to Tullochgorm

Davochs 1773

Davoch of Muckerach

Milntown of Muckerach, Corn Milne of Muckerach, Belnain, Muckerach, Breas of Muckerach, Auchguchule of Muckerach, Wester Achnahannet, Rynrich improvement (later in Tullochgribben davoch), Lagnasleach improvement, Correskaich improvement, Clachglass improvement, Rychraggan improvement, Lynlish and Old Castle of Muckerach.

Davoch of Finlarg

Easter Achnahannet, Wester Finlarg, Auchtocork, Wester Finlairg, Easter Finlairg, Croft of Achnahoilt.

Davoch of Curr

Lands of Easter and Wester Curr, Glengour, Improvement of Rycorrach

Davoch of Clowrie

Clowrie

Davoch of Tullochgorm

Tullochgorm, Tiriebeg, Correchearcle

Allt Mor: Large stream NH 9703 2731 Meikle Burn 1770, Ault Nea More 1809.

A burn formed by the Allt Tarsuinn and Rychraggan Burn. Its course is short, being not more than a mile. [OSNB]

Allt Tarsuinn: The transverse or crosswise burn NH 9669 2908 Burn of Cuarst an Tarson 1767, Ault Tarson 1809.

A small burn rising from a green hollow between Creagan an Righ and Cam Sgriob, joining with Rychraggan Burn to form the burn known as Allt Mor. [OSNB]

Auchnahailt: 1808 Field of limestone NH 9865 2617 1841 see Auchnapoit.

Auchnahannet: Field of the chapel Auchnahandycht 1611, Achnahannit Roy, Achnyhannet 1767, Achnahanat 1841, Auchnahandycht 1841, Achnahannat 1851, Achnahannet 1871

Applied to five steadings with suitable out offices, they are each one storey high, thatched and in good repair. [OSNB]

Auchnahannet: NH 9767 2723

Fields: Bard Beg, The Dreim, Coul n Ty, Crait Vein, Torron a Luack, Tor du. 1809

Auchnahannet: NH 9766 2776

Fields: Tor du, Cuach Lar, Bruich n Ty, Bruach Ual, Dike Cloigh. 1809

Auchnahannet: NH 9749 2772

Fields: Fiachin-Cruy, The Crait, Dreiman Loch, Bruich-n-leis, Staultua. 1809

Auchnahannet: NH 9731 2736

Auchnahannet: NH 9758 2667 Green Gutter

Auchnahannet Burn: NH9732 2721

A large burn rising near to Easter Ryneckra and flowing in a south westerly direction until it joins the River Dulnain, near to the Mill of Muckrach. It also formed part of the boundary between the parish of Duthil and Rothiemurchus, and the parish of Cromdale, Inverallan and Advie. [OSNB]

Auchnahannet Chapel (possible site NH 9750 2701)

Fields: Chappellhow 1770, Chappell Well 1770.

Nothing is known about the history of this early Christian site.

Auchnapoit: 1767 Field of the pot NH 9865 2617 AuchnyPeot 1767.

On 1767 map, an established improvement on east side of Scumaraid, near track to Finlurg and Brae of Muckrach. The field is shaped like a pot. Later appears to be renamed, see Auchnahailt.

Cairn of Achnyhyle: 1767 Hill of the limestone field NH 9864 2670 Hill of Achnyhyle 1770.

Hill behind Auchnahailt.

Bachk Buie: 1809 Yellow bank NH 9535 2962

Appears to be the previous name for Craig an Righ. The western end of Craig an Righ was Bachk Buie and the eastern side Craig Sluigh.

Ball a Chruichk: 1808   Farmstead of the knoll, heap, rounded hill set apart   NH 9838 2511   Town of Bella Chliechk 1767, Ball a Chruichk 1808, Knock of Muckrach, Muckrach Farm.

Old name for Muckrach farm.

Fields: Chapple Field, Lack Vouie, Bruich More, Croumoran. 1808

Ballintomb Pictish Stone: NH 995 253   Class 1 Pictish symbol stone, built into the garden wall of Finlarig House. Stone was found at Ballintomb farm cottages being used as a flagstone. Stone has a crescent and V-rod with a 'tuning fork' and mirror. Possibly linked to site of earlier standing stones at Ballintomb.

Balnaan: x2   Farmstead by the ford   NH 9791 2495, NH 9765 2471 Belnaun 1611, Bellenaan 1767, 1841, Balnain 1851, Balnan 1871, South Balnain 1871.

Two croft houses one north and the other south of the River Dulnain, with suitable offices, one storey high, thatched and in good repair. [OSNB]

Fields Upper Balnaan: The Haugh, Toum Baan. 1808

Ballechule: Corner or back farmstead and corner field   NH 9787 2524   Ball a Chuil 1808, Auchkacoul 1767, Oachkacoul 1767, Ouchhachoul 1767, Auchguchule 1773

Balnabrick: Not located on maps apart from Roy's. In Balnacruie, Croftnahaven area on Roy's map.

Balnacroigh: Farmstead of the tree   NH 9701 2246   Ballnakree Roy, Ballnacruie 1810, Balnacraibh 1841, Upper Balnacruie, Upper Balnacrie 1860, Upper Balnacraoibh 1861.

A small farmsteading, dwelling house one storey & offices all in a very bad state of repair. [OSNB]

Lower Balnacruie: 1810   NH 9719 2245   Ballnakree Roy, Balnacreigh 1851.

A middling sized farm steading consisting of a very good dwelling house and a good set of offices. One storey all thatched and in fair state of repair. [OSNB]

Balnuichk: The farmstead on the face of the hill   NH 9862 2589

Ballnuichk 1841, Balnuchk 1851 Balnuchk, Balnuick, Balnuchd 1861, Balnochd 1901.

A farmhouse and offices one storey high thatched and in good repair. [OSNB]

Fields: Ochku Hius, Stob Meugh, Gorstan a Gouram, Ochku Meinach, Ochku Rossich

Balvattan: Farmstead of the little clumps   NH 9669 2223 Belvattan 1771, Ballavattan of Tullochgorm 1795, Ballawaden 1810, Balwattan 1841.

A small farmsteading, dwelling house one storey thatched, having a small court of offices, a short distance from the dwelling house, all in a fair state of repair. The small farm of Broompark lying a short distance west of this one is now let with it and the two form one holding. [OSNB]

Field: The Cruichan 1810

Balvattan Beg: Little farmstead of the clumps   NH 9681 2240

Bardbially: Appears in 1841 census between Ochnoir and Balvattan. Not located on a map.

Bardnastri: Appears in 1841 census between Torrispardon and Clury. Not located on a map.

Bat Eagh: 1809   Place of horses   NH 9631 2747.

Beum a'Chlaidheimh: Stroke of the sword NH 9371 3071 Vhein a Chlay 1809, Bhem a Chlav 1809.

A deep hollow or pass through which the road from Carrbridge to Forres and Nairn passes. [OSNB] Also the name given to the hill on the east overlooking it. According to local folklore and the Old Statistical Account, the gash in the rocks was caused by a Fingalian giant, who in frustration while hunting, dashed his sword into the hill with a mighty blow.

Blaar Tor Du: 1808   Black or dark hill moss   NH 9858 2755

Broomhill Station: 1871   NH 9955 2260

Opened in 1863 by Inverness & Perth Junction Railway and later became the Highland Railway. 51 miles from Inverness and 92 miles from Perth. [OSNB] It closed under the Beeching cuts in 1965 and since 2002 is run by Strathspey Railway.

Broompark: NH 9630 2212   Broom Park 1771, Broom Waird 1810.

Two small houses occupied by labouring men, each one storey, thatched and in middling repair. The place was once a farmtown, but is now let with the farm of Balvattan. [OSNB]

Field: Deers Know 1771

Field: Lag Shellach 1810

Bruntland: 1810   Burnt land   NH 9759 2353

Cairn Glass: 1807   Grey cairn   NH 9714 2417   Cairn of Clurie 1767, Cairn Glass Park 1807

Bronze Age cairn with views north and west over the River Dulnain. Eroded due to agricultural activity.

Cairn n Oig: 1808   Hill of the champion or youth   NH 998 254

Cam Sgriob: Crooked furrow   NH 9749 3015   Caunscriep 1809, Kaunscriep 1809.

A prominent hill on the same ridge and about a mile eastward of Creag an Righ. The former county boundary between Inverness-shire and Moray, once passed over the summit. [OSNB] It's now on the northern boundary of the Cairngorms National Park. The furrows on the summit are striations caused by melt water streams under the moving ice sheet.

Caochan Ban: White burn   NH 9790 2864

A small burn having its source at the base of the range of hills over which the former boundary of the parish crossed, and flowing in a westerly direction until it joins Achnahannet Burn near to Clachbain farmhouse. [OSNB]

Caochan Ruadh: Red burn   NH 9781 2739

A small burn having its source at the western base of the Beinn Mhor. Formed the eastern boundary of the parish, and flows in a south westerly direction until it joins Achnahannet Burn, near to the most southern former farmhouse of Achnahannet. [OSNB]

Carn Elric: Hill of the deer trap or rocky sloped hill   NH 9431 3047   Vhinn a Chlay 1809, Vhem a Clav, Creag Ealraich

A prominent hill situated with rocky outcrops on its southern sides.

[OSNB] Known on older maps as Beum a'Claidheimh. Now on the boundary of the Cairngorms National Park.

Carn Sliak: 1767   Hill of the pass between two hills   NH 9598 3012

Refers to the track which rises from Auchnahannet to Lochindorb to the west of Cam Sgriob. Carn Sliak is not shown on modern Ordnance Survey maps. It is the eastern end of Creag and Righ, facing Cam Sgriob.

Craig of Slioch: 1767   Craig of the pass or hollow   NH 9620 3016
Craig of Sluich 1767.

On eastern end of hill now known as Creag an Righ.

Burn of Sluik: 1767   Burn of the pass or hollow   NH 9650 2933

Caultersneigh: 1809   Possibly Cuil Tire, secluded land   NH 9599 2715

A moss east of Rueruich.

Caultersneigh Beg: 1809   NH 9629 2850

Chappelfield: 1767   NH 2995 8254

Enclosure around Finlarig chapel.

Chappell: 1767   NH 9931 2542

Remains of medieval chapel & cemetery at Finlarig with rectangular earth walls within circular enclosure. Pictish Class 1 stone in National Museum of Scotland and on loan to Grantown Museum, found on west side of enclosure. Little is known about the chapel, other than the lands were once owned by the Bishops of Moray.

Chapellhow: 1770   NH 949 270

From place name evidence, the location of the former chapel of Achnahannet. Nothing is known about this religious settlement.

Chappell Well: 1770   NH 949 270

Implies association with site of Achnahannet Chapel.

Clach Baan: 1809   White stone   NH 980 287

Standing stone in a field to the east of Clachbain farm. According to a clause in the tenant's lease, he had to keep the upright stone in the middle of the field painted white. It might have originally been called Clach Glass (Grey stone).

Clachbain: White stone   NH 9793 2879   1851, 1901

A farm steading and outoffices one storey high, thatched and in good repair. [OSNB]

This was possibly also known as the improvement of Clachglass, which appears in early rentals but Clachbain does not. They would appear to have been in the same vicinity.

Claggin: 1801   NH 9942 2544

A former small farmhouse west of Finlarig House. Name for best arable field on a farm or a rounded hillock. Can also mean a small hand bell. Possibly a connection with the former Finlarig chapel.

Clury: The meadow   NH 9701 2377   Klour Pont, Clowrie 1611, Clurie 1704, Roy, Mains of Clury 1810, House of Clury 1841, Clury House 1871.

A farm steading dwelling house and offices, from one to two stories high, partly slated and partly thatched, in good repair. [OSNB]

Fields: Cairnfield, Ouchk Chlerich, Moss of Clurie, Parks of Clurie, The Back of the Town, Creit Dow, Crockan Cruie, 1767

Fields: Cairn Glass Park, Rieclairch Park, Turnip Park, Limekiln Park, Town Park, Garden Park, Lower Presintoul, Upper Presintoul, Black Park 1807

Field: Reiclairoch Park, Turneep Park, Limekiln Park, Cairn Glass Park, Cairn Glass, Town Park, Garden Park, Black Park, Lower Presintoul, Upper Presintoul 1810

Moss of Clurie: 1767   NH 9766 2379

Coldholme: 1841   NH 9968 2634

A small dwelling house one storey high, with offices attached, the whole thatched and only in middling repair. [OSNB]

Corr Our Vhem: 1809   Dun coloured corrie of Beum a' Chlaidheimh NH 9456 3039

Craggan-na-Narach: 1809   Little rocks of the adder   NH 9556 3108

Creag Bheag: Small crag   NH 9813 2816

Applied to a rocky area south east of Clachbain and overlooking the track from Upper Achnahannet. [OSNB]

Creag Mhor: Large crag   NH 9677 2302

A hill over which the former boundary between the parishes of Duthil and Rothiemurchus and part of Cromdale, Inverallan and Advie in the County of Inverness met. [OSNB]

Creag an Righ: Craig of the king   NH 9553 2977   Creag an Righ, Craig Gauleloch 1809, Bachk Buie 1809

A rugged hill over which the former boundary between Moray and the County of Inverness ran.   [OSNB] On older maps appears as Bachk Buie and the current name instead of 'the king' could be in error for ruighe. Creag an Ruighe, The shieling crag. Both the former shielings of Rychraggan and Rynruich are close by. Now on the boundary of the Cairngorms National Park.

Crochkan Buie: 1801   Yellow crooked field   NH 9934 2550

A field on Claggin farm.

Croftdow: Black Croft   NH 9756 2296   Roy, Croft Dow 1810, Croftow 1841, Farm of Croftdow 1841

A farmhouse and steading one storey, thatched and in good repair. [OSNB]

Field: Touperaie 1810

Croftdow Croft: NH 9745 2268

Croftjames: NH 9713 2280   Creit James 1771, Croft James 1810, Crofthemish, Clurie 1840, Crofthemish of Clury 1841, 1850, Croftjames 1871.

Fields: Meikle Brae, Dachafatta, Cairn Nicol, Toupernachyle 1771

This name is applied to a number of crofters' houses each one storey, all thatched and in a fair state of repair. There is a smithy and a joiner's shop included in the number. [OSNB]

In a few records appears as Crofthemish.

Croftnahaven: Croft of the river   NH 9810 2212, NH 9791 2204, NH 9866 2235, NH   Easter Cruitnahaun Roy, Creitnahawen 1771, Creithawen 1771, Creitenhawen 1767, Croftnahaven 1810, Crofthaun 1851.

This name applies to three small farmhouses each one storey high, thatched and in bad condition. [OSNB]

Field: Yellow How 1767

Fields: Little Haugh, Yellow How, Island Leys, Hard Hillock, Back of the Kiln, Black Croft, Meadow Rigs, Meikle Haugh, The Oxgang 1771

Croftnahaven Plantation: NH 9774 2230

Cural Brae na Laggan: 1808   NJ 0016 2627

On southern slope of Laggan Hill, near source of Laggan Burn.

Cur Skaich: 1767   Shady corrie   Corseaich 1767, Chor Skaich 1809, Cor Skaich 1809.

An isolated improvement on the watershed with Dava Moor.

Easter Curr: East corner   NH 9978 2411   NH 9982 2416   Eister Cure 1611, Easter Curr Roy, Cure 1702, Nether Cure 1703, Easter Cur 1810, East Curr 1841.

A dwelling house and out offices one storey high, thatched and in good repair. [OSNB]

Fields: Upper Wyndings, Meikle Torgarrow, Little Torgarrow, Kiln Drum, Townack, Lagliea, Mid Wyndings, Haugh of Easter Curr 1771

Mid Curr: Mid corner   NH 9974 2347, NH 9966 2381   Mid Cur 1810

Applies to two farmhouses and offices one storey high, thatched and in good condition. [OSNB]

Mains of Curr: NH 9941 2265

Previously Wester Curr

Moss of Curr: 1771   NH 9927 2398

Wester Curr: West corner   NH 9941 2265   Wester Cure 1611, Wester Curr Roy, Wester Cur 1810, West Curr 1841, Mains of Curr 1901.

A farmhouse and steading, former one storey high and thatched, latter one storey also, but slated and in very good condition. [OSNB]

Fields: Meikle Haugh or Dellmore, Little Haugh, Waterside, Ellon 1767

Fields: Goat's Croft, Delmore, Haugh of Curr, Easter Haugh of Curr, Commonty, Back of Victual House, Ellon 1771

Curr Wood: Corner wood   NH 9941 2322

A large pine wood between Wester Curr and Skye of Curr.

Skye of Curr: Winged corner   NH 9907 2421   Karr, Pont, Meikle Skey 1810, Skey of Curr 1841, 1871.

This name applies to a line of very small farm houses, each of which is one storey high, thatched and in bad repair. [OSNB]

Little Skey: 1767   NH 9923 2303   Cairn Shea Chure 1767

 A hill above the Aviemore-Grantown road near Broomhill.

Meikle Skey: 1771   NH 9934 2247

A hill below the Aviemore-Grantown road near Broomhill.

Cairn at Skye of Curr Woods: NH 9951 2332

An ancient cairn supposed to have been erected either in the Pictish or Druidical era. It is composed of loose stones and is of considerable magnitude. When opened (1866) for antiquarian purposes, two stone cists were found embedded among fine sand. [OSNB] A Bronze Age cairn within the wood behind the former Auchendean Lodge Hotel.

Dale Loupack: 1807   Field of the curve or bend   NH 9705 2469

Above Balnaan, where the River Dulnain forms a loop.

Dale Naan: 1807   Field by the ford   NH 9780 2470

Dreim a du: 1809   Black ridge   NH 9716 2707

Drynach: Place of thorns   NH 9741 2324   Drynnachan 1810, Drynach 1841,

Fields: Touperai, Cruitnaha 1767

Fields: Croftdow, Touper Eye 1810

A farmhouse steading and offices, one storey high thatched and in good repair. [OSNB]

Dulnan Bridge: NH 9968 2487   Bridge of Cur, Bridge of Dulnon 1771, Dulnain Bridge

A substantial stone bridge spanning the River Dulnan, about half a mile from its junction with the River Spey and on the road from Grantown to Aviemore. It is a County Bridge. [OSNB] The first bridge built in 1754 and rebuilt in 1791, was subsequently destroyed by flooding in 1829. Current bridge completed in 1830.

Now Dulnain Bridge.

Dulnanbridge: 1841   NH 9977 2489   Drochaid Thuilnean, Dulnain Bridge

A few dwelling houses at Dulnan Bridge, from which they take their name, one storey high thatched and in good repair. [OSNB] Now Dulnain Bridge.

Church Place: NH 9987 2485

Curr Road: NH 9968 2480

Fraser Road: NH 9961 2484

School Road: NH 9962 2478

School Place: NH 9953 2479

Skye of Curr Road: NH 9926 2464

Dulnan Bridge Post Office: NH 9980 2487

A dwelling house two stories high and used as Post Office and shop. It is subject to the Grantown Post Office Arrival 3 pm, Dispatch 10:30 am. [OSNB]

Dulnan Bridge School: NH 9962 2474

A plain substantial building to which is added a teacher's residence. It is one of the parish schools of the united parishes of Cromdale, Advie and Inverallan. Average attendance about 50 pupils. [OSNB] Built in 1890 it closed in 1960.

Dulnain Bridge Church: NH 9984 2492

Dulnain Bridge Old Tin Church: NH 9968 2477

Erected from corrugated iron in 1914, for the Established Church of Scotland.

Dulnain Bridge Hall & Institute: NH 9985 2490

Opened in 1896.

Dulnain Bridge Limekiln: NH 9986 2500

A large limekiln built in 1787 for limestone, quarried on slopes of Laggan Hill. This was used for fertiliser and mortar for building.

Dulnainbridge Plantation: NH 9954 2509

River Dulnan: Floody river   NH 9945 2492   Tuilnean, Dulnen

Water (Pont), Water of Dulnon 1771, Dulnan River 1801, Water of Dulnan 1810, River Dulnain.

A small river which has its source in several head streams rising in the hills between Craig Alvie and the head of the River Findhorn. Its course is easterly, passing the village of Carr Bridge onto the River Spey, into which it empties itself a short distance below the farm steading of Ballintomb. [OSNB]

Fait Vait: 1809   Submerged bog stream   NH 9686 2734

A worn out peat moss.

Fea Buie: 1809   Yellow bog stream   NH 9724 2690

Findlarigg: White or holy pass   NH 9944 2533   Finlarig Roy 1871, Finlairge 1704, Findlarig 1841, Findlarg 1851, Ovir Finlairge 1611, Nether Finlairge 1611, Mains of Findlarig 1901, Over Finlarig alias Mukrothe.

A large house, two storeys high, with offices attached, the former slated, the latter thatched, the whole in thorough repair. [OSNB]

Fields: Bruich Beg, Bruich More

Findlarigg Burn: NH 9920 2595   Finlarig Burn

A small burn which rises about half a mile north west of Coldhome and runs in a southern direction until it flows into the River Dulnain, a short distance below Muckrach Lodge. Former county boundary between Inverness-shire and Moray. [OSNB]

Finlarig Pictish Stone: Ballintomb Pictish Stone   NH 995 253

Class 1 Pictish symbol stone. Built into the garden wall Finlarig House. Stone was found at Ballintomb farm cottages being used as a flagstone. Stone has a crescent and V-rod with a 'tuning fork' and mirror. Possibly linked to earlier standing stone at Ballintomb.

Finlarig Chapel Pictish Stone: NH 9891 2536   Pictish Class 1 symbol stone of mica schist incised on one face with a divided rectangle and Z rod over a crescent and V rod. Now on display in Grantown Museum.

Green Gutter: NH 9758 2667   Another name for the lowest Auchnahannet. Little now remains apart from a gable wall.

Laggan of Findlarigg: NH 9922 2578   Finlarig 1808, Laggan of Findlarig 1851, Upper Findlarig 1901.

A farm house, one storey high with numerous offices attached, thatched and in fair repair. [OSNB]

Fields: The Kiln Park, Bruich More, Park Lackan Beg, Park Torron Lein, Park Lackan Du, Upper Park, Slachken Ruich. 1808

Finlarig Wood: NH 9978 2546

Easter Laggan: The little hollow   NJ 0031 2567   Upper Laggan Roy, Laggan 1841

A large farm steading dwelling house, one storey and offices are all thatched and in a bad state of repair. There are a few small cot houses on this farm occupied by labouring men. [OSNB]

Fields: Stau n Doul, Stau na Criu Curan. 1808

Wester Laggan: Little hollow   NH 9999 2533   Lower Laggan 1851

A farmhouse one storey high, with a cottar's dwelling house and offices attached, thatched and in fair repair. [OSNB]

Laggan Burn: Burn of the little hollow   NJ 0019 2522

A small burn, rising about half a mile to the north of Wester Laggan farmhouse and flowing in a south eastern direction for about 2 miles, where it joins the River Spey. [OSNB]

Laggan Hill Cup Marked Stones: NH 9995 2595

Several boulders and outcrops of rock on south western slopes of Laggan Hill have numerous cup marks cut in the stone, dating from the Bronze Age.

Laggan Lime Stone Quarries: NH 999 262

During the 18th and 19th century, limestone was quarried on Laggan Hill for agricultural fertiliser and mortar for building. The quarries are still visible on the southern slopes.

Leachkin Du Auchnahailt: 1808   Slope of the limestone field NH 9876 2688

Lieachcu: NH 9678 2256   Liechlew 1771, Knock Greslach 1771

Loch Beum a'Chlaidheimh: Loch of the stroke of the sword NH 9376 3029   Lochanbem Roy, Loch a Viem 1809, Loch a Vhem 1809.

A small loch on the east side of the road leading from Carrbridge to Forres and Nairn. [OSNB] It's named after the pass of Beum Chlaidheimh.

Lochindorb Road: 1809   NH 9736 2952   Hill track from Clachbain to west end of Lochindorb.

Loch na Stewartack: 1809   Loch of the black headed gull   NH 9710 2787

Lyneleish: Enclosed meadow   NH 9883 2502   1841, Lynelish Roy, Linelishmore 1767, Lenleish, 1801, Linlish 1801, Lyne Leish 1808

Fields: Crait na Garnal, Dale Tau, Dale Gannich, Ochku Hius, Ochku Meinach, Stob Fleugh, Gartan Gour, Caulterneigh, Lyneleish more 1808

Meaul Rheaur: 1808   Large, plump hill   NH 9944 2701

A rounded hill whose name does not appear on modern maps.

Military Road Aviemore to Grantown: 1807   NH 9799 2297

Muckrach: Place of the pigs

Braes of Muckrach: Brae of the place of the pigs   NH 9845 2575   1871, Braes of Muckrach 1611, Braes of the Town 1767, Brae Muckerach 1808, Braes of Mukrach 1841, Upper Muckrach 1901

Fields: Dreiman Shogle, Lak Vouie, Auch Crascach. 1808

Muckrach Castle: NH 9858 2505   Muckrach Pont, Mukrauche 1611, Muckrach Castle Roy, Mikrath 1841, Muckrach 1851,

A ruin situated about ¼ mile north of Muckrach House. It was erected by the Grants of Rothiemurchus in 1598. It is now in a very serious condition. Nothing remains of it except the walls. [OSNB]

Built by Patrick, second son of John Grant of Freuchie and the original seat of the Grants of Rothiemurchus. It fell into ruin until restored by Ian Begg from 1978-1985. Now let for holiday accommodation.

Mill of Muckrach: 1611   NH 9753 2487   Mill of Mukrach 1841

Applied to a corn mill- farmhouse and out offices, each of which are one storey high, thatched and in good repair. [OSNB] see Mullenphenachan.

Milton of Muckrach: NH 9732 2513   Miltown 1611, Miltown 1841, Miltown of Muckrach 1861.

A farmhouse and outoffices one storey high, thatched and in good repair. [OSNB]

Fields: Crait Cruy, The Haugh. 1808

Muckrach Castle

Muckrach Farm: See Ball a Chruichk and Knock of Muckrach

Muckrach Lodge: NH 9889 2504   Muckrach House, Muckrach 1871, Muckrach Country House Hotel

An elegantly built house two storeys high with coach house and other out houses attached, the former slated and in excellent condition, the latter thatched and in good repair. [OSNB] Now the Muckrach Country House Hotel.

Knock of Muckrach: Hillock of the place of pigs   NH 9838 2511 Town of Bella Chliechk 1767, Ball a Chruichk 1808, Muckrach Farm

A farmhouse and outoffices one storey high, thatched and in good repair. [OSNB]

Mullenphenachan: Mill of the crow   Mulnphenachan, Mulafeanach Roy, Mulnfenichan 1838, Mulnfenchan 1840, Mill-town of Mulnfenchan, Mullinfenchan 1901, Mill of Clurie 1807

became Mill of Muckrach.

Nea Vouie: 1808 Sacred place NH 9769 2614 Neavouie

Ochnoir: Slope of gorse, whins, earlier Gorse Hillock NH 9628 2191 Ouchkenir 1771, Oughtanoir 1771, Knock an Oire of Tullochgorm 1809, Oucheanaur 1810, Uchdnoir 1841, Ucuneir 1851, Uchdanoir 1871, Ocknoir 1860.

Two small farm houses with a lot of small offices, each one storey high, thatched and in middling repair. A short distance west from these farmhouses, in a birch wood, there is a wooded pulpit resembling a sentry box, with a small open space around it, open air preachings are held here occasionally in the summer season by the Free Church Minister of Duthil. [OSNB]

Adjacent property called Broompark.

Fields: Fernabrogue, Little Reeganny, Broom Know, Hen's Croft 1771

Fields: Ri Canny, Criecht More, Lag Shellach 1810

Ouchkuchlorich: Hill side of the clerk or clergyman   NH 9812 2444 Roy, Ouchan Chlerich 1767

Primrose Wood: NJ 0005 2541

Once a popular haunt in spring with a yellow carpet of flowers.

Rôches Moutonnées: Sheep back   NJ 0003 2501

A rock formation caused by the passing of a glacier, eroding the underlying bed rock in the ice age. Named after the 18th century French style of wig smoothed with mutton fat, which the formation resembled.

Rycraggen: Shieling of the little rocks   NH 9485 2952   Rue Craggan 1809, Recraggan 1851.

An old house and a number of ruins. All the remains of a farm house and steading. [OSNB]

Rychraggan Burn: Burn of the shieling of the little rocks   NH 9617 2793

A small burn gathering in the moss a little to the west of Creag an Righ. It served as parish boundary to Tom Eiridh, then easterly until it's joined by Allt Tarsuinn. [OSNB]

Rynruich: Heather shieling   NH 9528 2857   Rien Ruick 1767,

Rue n Ruich 1809, Ruen-Ruich 1860

A small farmhouse with suitable offices attached, one storey high and in bad repair. [OSNB] At various times was part of Muckrach davoch and then Tullochgribben.

Rynruich

Scumban Ard: 1808   Height of the white hillock   NH 9825 2662 Hill of Scumarard 1767, Toumban Ard 1808.

Sleigh: The hollow or pass NH 9648 2923 Improvement of Sleuich 1767, Sluich 1767, Sluigh 1809

The meaning of this word is obscure, it is applied to a shealling which consists of ruins of houses and sheep folds. [OSNB]

Strun Daie: 1809   NH 9651 3020

Tombuie: 1771   Yellow hillock   NH 9850 2241

A moor, now planted behind Croftnahaven.

Tom Eiridh: Rising knoll NH 9579 2783 Touman Eirreri 1809

A slope rising from the south side of the Rychraggan Burn. [OSNB]

Torgarve: The rough hill

Mentioned close to Lynleish, but not located on maps.

Torrispardan: Hillock with the flat top or level side, the roosting hill   NH 9696 2336   Town of Torspardon 1767, Torspartan 1810, Torsparden 1810, Torispardon 1901.

This name is now given to two small farm steadings (which are let under one). The houses are each one storey, offices one, all thatched and middling repair. [OSNB]

Toum Cairn: Cairn hillock. NH 9601 2173 [OSNB]

A fine Bronze Age cairn 4m high, with commanding views to south and east over Strathspey. On the former boundary with Duthil parish.

Toum a Vaich: 1809   Hillock of the byre   NH 9791 2923

Brae of Tulloch: Roy   Fields rising from the main road to the hill ridge overlooking Tullochgorm.   NH 9646 2205

Tullochgorm: Blue green hillock   NH 9693 2133 Tullochgorme Pont, Tullouchgorme 1611, Tullochgoram Roy, 1810, Tulloch Gorm 1703, Mains of Tullochgorm 1771, Tullochgorm 1841, Tullochgorum 1871.

A large farmsteading one of the best in the neighbourhood, the dwelling house is two storeys, slated with a good court, offices one storey all in first rate repair, occupied by Mr D Grant, farmer. This is the place from which the famous Strathspey Tullochgorum, takes its name. [OSNB]

Fields: Garden, Haugh Ground, Chappell Leys, Long Leys, Barn Hill, Cott Fold. 1771

Cottar Town Fields: Sutors Hillock, Broom Hillock, Lands of Reegany. 1771

Fields: Easter Haugh, Garden, Wester Haugh, Old Chapel, Chapel Field, Dorachoart, Brandy Well, Ri Canny.1810

Tullochgorm Cottage: NH 9711 2132

Tullochgorm Stone Circle: Tullochgorm Cairn   NH 9648 2131

A small piece of uncultivated land on which are ranged in a circle, a considerable number of stones of various dimensions. Very little is known about this object of antiquity in the locality. It however is generally believed to have originally been a Druidical place of worship and after the introduction of Christianity to have been used as a Christian place of worship and a sepulchre for the burial of unbaptised infants. [OSNB]

A Clava-type cairn, little remains complete of the cairn apart from the kerb and suggestions of a former enclosing stone circle.

Tullochgorm Standing Stones: NH 9670 2103

Two undressed stones of irregular form standing in a field, on the north side of the River Spey. The only tradition regarding them in the neighbourhood is, that they are believed to have been erected by the Picts for some particular purpose. [OSNB]

Standing stones possibly from the Bronze Age on farmland close to the River Spey. Stones are aligned to where the full moon can set around the spring and autumn equinoxes.

Waulk Mill: NH 9946 2494 Waulkmiln of Dulnan 1808

Waulkmill Croft: 1841   NH 9942 2497

Whitewell: 1851   NH 9695 2263   White Well 1861.

A small spring well, situated on the western croft of Croftjames. Provides an excellent supply in all seasons. [OSNB]

Walks

1: Tullochgorm to Balnaan

Standing in the field next to the two standing stones of Tullochgorm with its famous fiddle tune association with Strathspey, is as good a place as any to begin exploring the places and their names in the former parish of Cromdale, Inverallan and Advie. These stones erected by some of the earliest inhabitants of the area, long before the coming of Christianity would have looked on the same magnificient view south towards the Monadh Ruigh or Cairngorms. We don't know what they called them or even the language they used, but human nature being what it is, there must have been a name to identify them in conversation. Some of the earliest settlers probably during the Mesolithic period would follow the River Spey and its tributaries upstream from the coast of the Moray Firth or from the passes of Drumochter and Minnigaig to the south. Little archaeological exploration has been done in this area, but later peoples must have found the area agreeable for their needs and settled.

There are several surviving Bronze Age monuments on the lower reaches of the Spey within the parish. From Tullochgorm a path and farm road beside the Strathspey railwayline leads to the main road passing an old cairn. Looking up towards the Brae of Tulloch among the birch trees, the large cairn of Toum surveys the landscape beneath, as it's done for the last 2700-4000 years. Access can be made from the road to Ochnoir and following the tree line north towards Upper Balnacruie and Croft James. At Croft James taking the minor road due north to Balnaan, is the likely route followed by travellers for centuries. Here a bridge replaced a ford or ferry that crossed the River Dulnain. Before reaching the bridge, on the left the large 18th century Clury House is visible through the trees. This was the former home of the Grants of Clury, a cadet branch of Freuchie. A little further on the left within a field are the remains of Cairn Glass, a heavily eroded Bronze Age cairn. Crossing the bridge reaches the main road where the choice is to return the same way or push on to walks two and three.

2: Balnaan to Auchnahannet and Creag Ealrich

Beyond Balnaan the single track road continues in a straight line ever northwards to the farms of Auchnahannet, Clachbain and Rynechra. There are two locations within the parish that bear the name Auchnahannet. Both are early Celtic Christian sites and mean field of the church. The old maps pinpoint a Chapel Well and Howe, though no structural remains are visible. Nothing either is known about the history. Pushing on, the road becomes an untarred track towards Clachbain, leaving the arable land for the broad expanse of moor and rising rugged rocks of Cam Sgriob and Creag an Righ. Clachbain recently come back into habitation, sits by a standing stone of the same name. Seemingly a previous tenant as part of his tenancy had to paint the stone white. Thankfully it's now returned to its natural condition.

Options from here are: a track through the heather that skirts Cam Sgriob to the east and on to Lochindorb, continue towards Rynechra; or returning to Upper Auchnahannet a track heads west to Rynruich and Rycraggan. Both now in ruins, they are worth visiting as due to their remoteness they have retained many of their original features. Sheep tracks now climb upwards to the watershed at Corrour and the summit of Creag Ealrich. A rocky scree overlooks the road from Carrbridge to Nairn and Forres and according to legend was created by a giant with a strike of his sword. A great vantage point rewards the long walk in, with views stretching for miles.

3: Muckrach, Dulnain Bridge to Skye of Curr

Returning from Auchnahannet and A938 junction follow the road towards Dulnain Bridge. On the left just hidden from view is the fully restored Muckrach Castle. A fine example of a Scottish tower house brought back to life by the architect Ian Begg. Now let to visitors, it can be viewed by following a track from the rear entrance to Muckrach Lodge. Built for a younger son of the Laird of Freuchie, it later fell into ruin as that branch removed to Rothiemurchus, where they remain today. It's not until almost upon the castle, that its strong defensive location can be appreciated. Returning to the main road leads to Dulnain Bridge which until at least the

53

early 20th century was happy to be known as Dulnan. The intrusive 'i' was allegedly imposed by the post office.Turning left past the garage the road climbs past the old limekiln on the Finlarig road. Past lower Finlarig on the left are the remains of Finlarig chapel. Another site of early Christianity in this vicinity. An enclosing wall, possibly marks a cemetery and an outline of a rectangular building, likely the chapel, can still be seen. Views from here are back towards Muckrach Castle and over Clury.

Return through Dulnain Bridge to a circular route via Skye of Curr or Easter Curr. Skye of Curr was founded in 1796 when Sir James Grant offered leases along what was then the main road from Grantown to Aviemore. Strung out along the road many of the original houses and their fields can still be seen, though new builds are encroaching. Passing the Heather Centre back to the main road which on the right returns to Croft James junction or by going left for 250m on the main road, a stile gains access to the old road. The track eventually enters Curr wood and continues behind the quarry to regain the old road before Mid Curr. A detour to the old burial cairn behind Auchendean Lodge is worth a visit before passing Easter Curr where the choice is a footpath through the wood or by the new main road back to Dulnain Bridge.

Balvattan and Tullochgorm

Broomhill Station

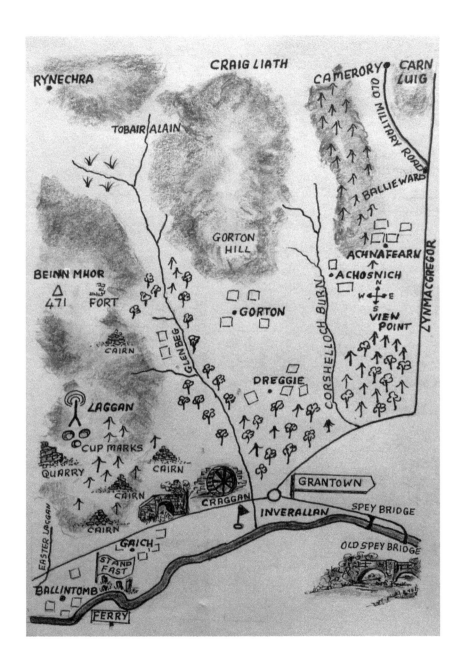

CHAPTER 2

Ballintomb, Glen Beg, Dreggie to Ballieward

Davochs 1773

Davoch of Ballintomb

Bellintomb & Bellintruan, Nether Laggan, Correnloch

Davoch of Gaich

Kirktown & Croft Farquhar, Gaich, Croft McEwan, Lochend of Gaich, Laggan, Ryneachrae, Dochnuaran improvement, Batchait improvement, Wester Crannich, Easter Crannich

Davoch of Dreggie

Achosnich, Easter & Wester Dreggies, Gortown, Lands of Kylintrae & Park of Duglaig, The New Park at Grantown.

Davich of Glenbegg 1773

Craggan, Waulk miln of Craggan, Tourannabirracks, Drumourachie, Glenbegg, Belnacoule,Rysaurie improvement, Drumvattan & Glaicknasovie, Shendale, Cairnglass, Ryluachrach, & Feabain, Tomnryrannich, Miln & Miln Croft of Craggan.

Achosnich: Field of sighing, groaning or blasts, gusts of wind NJ 0240 2941   Achosnich 1841, 1851, 1861, 1871, Achosnick,1901, Auchcosaniche 1611, Achosnich Roy, Auchorsnich 1767, Achosnach 1820,

A farmhouse and out offices from one to two storeys high, thatched and in good repair. [OSNB]

In the rental of 1611 this farm comprised of 4 oxgangs. Tenanted in 17th and 18th centuries by a Grant family of tacksmen, related to Tullochgorm Grants.

Fields: Lupeshalloch, Lands called Garroch, The Meikle Ley,How of the Barns, Land of Craggan More, Long Croft, Black Croft, Dyke Croft. 1767

Fields: The Upper Park, Gorstan Gorum. 1808

Allt Clais Bheithe: Burn of the birch gorge   NH 9866 3038 [OSNB]

Allt Clach na Saobhaidhe: x2 The burn of the stone of the fox. NH

9945 2955, NJ 0004 2894   Allt Glac na Saobhaidh, Glaichk na Suive 1808   Burn of the fox hollow.

A small burn having its source at the northern base of Beinn Mor and flowing in a south easterly direction until it joins Glenbeg Burn, near to Toumnarannich. [OSNB] On pre Ordnance Survey maps appears as Glac (hollow) rather than Clach (stone).

Allt Coire Buidhe: Burn of the yellow hollow   NJ 0078 3040

An Creagan: The small rock   NJ 0121 3006   Craggen Caash 1809

A small rocky hill situated immediately north of Carn a' Ghortein and on the same ridge. [OSNB]

Auchnafearn: Field of the alder   NJ 0282 2993   Achanafairn Pont, Auchnaphairn, Auchnaferne described as 'ane croft' in 1611 rental, Achnafairn Roy, Easter Achnafairn 1841, Wester Achnafairn 1841,1901, Achnafarn 1851, Achnafairn 1861, 1871, Auchnafarn 1770, Auchnyfearn 1767, Auchnafairn 1809,(Town of Auchnafern Easter & Wester Tack, Big Croft, Little Croft 1765)

A farmhouse and outoffices, one storey high slated, and in good repair. [OSNB]

Field Name: The Black Ward

Auchnafearn Wood: NJ 0246 2997

Hill of Auchnafern: 1765   Hill of the alder tree   See Carn Buidhe

Ballacha: Farmstead of the pass or road   Belcha 1851,

A croft house with suitable outoffices, one storey high thatched, and in good repair. [OSNB]

(Easter Ballacha) NJ 0256 3080

(Wester Ballacha) NJ 0262 3069

The pass runs between Craigbae and Carnluicht and was used by cattle drovers and then converted to a military road by Major Caulfeild.

Ballieward: The high farmstead or farmstead of the enclosed meadow   NJ 0281 3104   Belliward 1841, Lots of Belliward 1810 Belliward 1851, Ballieward 1861, Lots of Ballieward 1810 Balliward 1871, House of Bellieward 1765, Bellieward 1812, Belliward 1809,

Belleward 1770, Little Bellieward 1801 Belliward Tack

Applies to a district consisting of farm house and a number of croft houses. They are from one to two storeys high, thatched and in good repair. [OSNB]

Ballintomb: Farmstead of the hillock   NJ 0049 2460   1841

A farm house and out offices each of which is one storey high, partly slated and partly thatched, all in good repair. [OSNB]

Old Ballintomb: NJ 0087 2467   Belnatolme 1611, Bellintome 1703, Wester Ballintom Roy, Bellintom 1771,

Fields: The Park, The Grey Parks, Ryganny, The Kiln Kavell, The Pool, Allandu, Reefad, Cairnland, Pellindean. 1767.

Fields: The Park, The Gray Park, Rycanny, The Angle, Reefad, Kill Kavel, Pellendea, The Pool, Tornagarach, Moss of Bellintomb, The Knows. 1771

Fields: Stau Cairn Glas, Hauch land, Poul 1808

This place was once a large farm steading. It is now attached to the farm of Ballintomb, the houses are unoccupied and have been in ruins for a length of time. The present occupier of Ballintomb farm (Mr Stuart) says he will have them taken away, probably next year, and the ground occupied by them turned into arable lands. [OSNB]

Cross of Ballintomb: NJ 0113 2460   Cross shape feature cut in the ground beside the standing stones. Not shown on maps and no oral tradition as to its purpose. Human remains were found close-bye in 1836, when a trench was cut across Tom na Carragh. The Regality Court would assemble here to dispense justice and a gallows was also in the vicinity.

Moor of Bellintomb: NJ 0085 2495   Moss of Bellnatomb 1767

Ballintomb Wood: NJ 0003 2481

Ball na Cuil: 1809 Farmstead of the nook NJ 0045 2881 Belnacoul 1770, Ballnacuil 1808

Fields: The Duchachk, Barn Hillock, Haugh Ground, Drummore, Lauch Carry. 1771

Fields: Sochkach, Gorstan Ashach, Dale Rioch. 1808

Beachan (The):   Little birch wood   NJ 0209 2716   see Carna Veachan

Beinn Mhor: The large hill   NH 9936 2810   Hill of Binny More 1770, Bein a More 1808 [OSNB]

Rising to 471 m (1545 ft), this is the largest hill in terms of area, but not height, in the parish of Inverallan. It overlooks Glen Beg and has commanding views over Strathspey and the Cairngorms. Once the boundary between the counties of Moray and Inverness passed at its western foot. There is a trig point at the summit.

Beinn Mhor Cairn: NH 9977 2773

A burial cairn with central cist overlooking Glen Beg. The cairn has been plundered for stone for the construction of the adjoining Cairnglass improvement in the 18th century.

Belnatrowne: 1611   Farmstead of the streamlet   NJ 0039 2444 Balindruan 1702, Baletruan 1702, Bellintruan 1703, Ballintruan Roy, Bellnatrowen 1767, Belnatruan 1771.

Located to the west of Ballintomb, it no longer appears on modern Ordnance Survey maps.

Blaar na Payn: 1808   NH 995 298

Bruich na Strie: 1809   NH 9981 3014

Cairn a Chural: NJ 0038 2671

Appears on old maps as the former name for Laggan Hill. Possibly hill of the paniers, from the shape of Laggan Hill and the lesser spur.

Cairnglass Improvement: 1771   NJ 0055 2773

Cairnluichk: Hill of the hollow   NJ 0300 3148

Applied to two croft houses each of which has suitable out offices, one storey high, thatched and in good repair. [OSNB]

Camerory: Curve or bend of the reddish shieling   NJ 0226 3133 1841, Rurory (Pont), Camerory 1770, Camerory 1770, Camarory 1809, Camerory 1810, Camrory 1851, Camrorie 1861,

A few small houses and farm house, situated about two miles north of Grantown. They are all one storey high, thatched and only in middling repair. [OSNB]

Upper Camerory: NJ 0210 3130

Caochan nan Gabhar: Goats stream   NJ 0121 2849

A small burn rising at Easter Gorton and flowing in a south westerly direction until it joins Glenbeg Burn near to Wester Gorton. [OSNB]

Carn a' Ghoirtein: Cairn of the little corn field or enclosure   NJ 0112 2954   Cairn of Gortown 1770, Cairn a Gorton 1809, Gorton Hill [OSNB]

Now known as Gorton Hill, it has recently been planted with mixed woodland.

Carn Buidhe: The yellow hill   NJ 0225 3020

A prominent hill whose eastern face is thickly wooded, situated between the farms of Corshelloch and Auchnaferan. [OSNB]

Cairn Luig: Hill of the den or hollow   NJ 0300 3148   Cairnluichk 1810, Carn Luig Plantation 1801, Carnluicht Wood 1801 [OSNB]

Now on the northern boundary of the Cairngorms National Park.

Carn Tornabirack: 1808   Hill of the knoll of the point or snout   NJ 006 262

Carna Veachan: 1809   Hill of the little birch wood   NJ 0209 2716
See The Beachen

Corr Ballnacuil: 1808   Corrie of the farmstead of the nook   NJ 000 288

Corr Buie: 1809   Yellow corrie   NJ 0100 3058

Corrybuie: Yellow corrie   NJ 0024 2716   Cornabuie 1770, Cornachbuie 1771

A hill improvement in 1771.

Corshellach: Willow hollow   NJ 0180 2986 1851, Improvements of Corshalloch 1767, Corshellach of Dreggie 1841

A croft house one storey high, thatched and in good repair. [OSNB]

Corshellach Burn: Willow hollow burn   NJ 0212 2898

A burn rising in the hollow between Creag Bheithe Mhor and Achosnich and flowing southward until it changes to the Kylintra Burn near Grantown. [OSNB]

Corshalloch of Gorton: 1770   NJ 0158 2945

A ruin on the eastern slope of Gorton Hill.

Coul Finian: 1808   NJ 002 279

Craggan Brechk: 1808   Stoney Brae   NH 986 289

Lower Craggan: Lower Craggan (Meal) Mill   NJ 0216 2621   1851

A large stone building two stories with two wooden buildings attached in the same buildings. There is a large dwelling house with a few offices a short distance east from the mill. The whole forms one holding and is in a fair state of repair. [OSNB]

Fields: Lack-n-tyan vaan, Knockan Du, Metan. 1808

Lower Craggan Carding Mill: 1901   NJ 0221 2621

A large stone building two stories, slated used as a Carding Mill (for wool only) driven by water power, there is sawing and turning machinery on the ground floor. The whole superintended by Mr Grant, who occupies a neat cottage one storey, slated and in good repair, a short distance from the Carding Mill. [OSNB]

Lower Craggan Fort: NJ 0214 2586

An Iron Age fort earthwork, straddling a scrub covered glacial ridge

Lower Craggan Smithy: NJ 0211 2610

A small farmsteading, dwelling house and storey office, all thatched and in a bad state of repair. [OSNB]

Upper Craggan: Little Rocks   NJ 0193 2632   Croft of Craigane 1611, Craggen 1770, Cragan 1841

A large first rate farmsteading consisting of a large dwelling house and a number of offices all thatched and in good repair. The present tenant is a merchant in Grantown and lets place at a high rent in summer season. [OSNB]

Fields: Yellow Hillock, Auchvallan, Lagmore. 1770

Fields: Knockan Yeorn, Auch Vattan, Bual More, Dale na Ha, Tor Gannaich, Crait Leannachan. 1808

Craggan Caash: 1809   NJ 0121 3006

Craggan Sands: NJ 023 257

Craig Bae: 1809   Birch rock   NJ 0200 3072

Craig na Heuler: 1809   Eagle craig   NJ 0118 2564 The Eagle's Craig 1770

Creag a'Bheinnein: Craig of the peak or craig of the little hill
NJ 0013 2844

A small hill spur situated at the south eastern base of Beinn Mor.
[OSNB]

Creag Bheithe Bheag: Small craig of the birch tree NJ 0141 3129
Creag Bheithe Bheag Wood

A small hill covered with pine trees and lying about half a mile to
the north east of Creag Liath. [OSNB] Situated on the northern
boundary of the Cairngorms National Park.

Creag Bheithe Mhor: Large craig of the birch tree NJ 0201 3072
Creag Bheithe Mhor Wood

A prominent hill, the top of which is covered with pine trees and
situated about half a mile south east of Creag Bheithe Bheag and
south of Camerory. [OSNB]

Creag Liath: The grey craig   NJ 0061 3126   Craig Liea 1809

A prominent hill 450m (1473 ft) covered with heathy pasture and
rather rocky on its south western slope. [OSNB] Seen from the Dava
Moor looking south, the northern boundary of the Cairngorms
National Park crosses the summit and follows the watershed to the
east and west.

Creag Liath Cave: NJ   0062 3138

A small rock shelter on the southern side of the summit

Croftfarqhar: 1770   NJ 0160 2692   Croft Ferquair 1611, Croft
Farokir Roy, Croft Farrachar 1809, Croit Farrachar 1809

Field: Kilnhow

Croft Miller: NJ 0193 2645   Croit Miller 1808

Field belonging to the miller at Craggan.

Croftskellich: The story teller's croft NJ 0084 2526   Croft Skalycht
1611, Croft Sheallech 1767, Croft Skelloch 1771, Crait Skealich 1808,
Croftskellach 1841, Croftschellach 1871, Croftskelloch 1901

A small dwelling one storey with offices in the same range, all
thatched and in bad repair. There is a small croft of arable land with
this house. [OSNB]

Fields: Slau Cairn Glass, Fioch More, Auch Vattan 1808

Dreggie: The place of thorns or blackthorn   Kildreke 1357-62, Drekky 1445, Dregy 1511, Dreigy 1583, Dragy 1611.

Easter Dreggie: NJ 0221 2866   1841 Easter Dreggie 1809, Easter Dreggy 1851

A farm house and out offices, one storey high thatched and in good repair [OSNB]

The old Easter Dreggie is the current Wester Dreggie or Mid Dreggie

Fields: Gorstan a Moin, Toum Baan. 1809

Mid Dreggie   NJ 0209 2843   Midd Dreggie 1809, Mid Dreggy 1851

Fields: The Weaver's Baulk, The Hazle Head, Goose Croft, The Barn Hill, The Yard Field, The Fail Croft, The Peat Fold, The Little Face, McKay's Brae.1767

Fields: Dreim Vore, Knockan Dour, Rue n Heish, Rioch, Bual Ard. 1809

A farm house and out offices, one storey high, thatched and in good repair. [OSNB]

Now known as Wester Dreggie, was the original Easter Dreggie. The old Wester Dreggie was located further west and is now in ruins.

Wester Dreggie: NJ 0176 2802   Dregiebeg Roy, Wester Driggy 1769, Wester Dreggie 1809   Also appears as Quarry Cottage on modern Ordnance Survey maps.

A farm steading consisting of dwelling house and office houses, one storey high, thatched and in bad condition. [OSNB] Now a ruin and not to be confused with current Wester Dreggie.

Fields: Dreim a Vriper, Dreim Vore 1809

Drumourachie: Ridge of the new field   NJ 0101 2750 Drumurchy Roy, Drimurachie 1770,

Dreim Urachy 1808

Fields: Back of the Yard, The Kavell, Wet Toths, Sheep's Croft, The Tormore. 1771

A one storey thatched dwelling house in very bad condition. [OSNB]

Dulaig Falls: The dark hollow water fall   NJ 0246 2833

Dulecht Bridge: NJ 0248 2827 Former railwaybridge crossing the road to Dreggie and Corshellach Burn.

Du Glaichk: 1809   The dark hollow   NJ 0218 2804   Dowleck 1767, The Park of Dulechk 1771   Dulaig Moss 1778, Park of Dulaig 1778, Dulicht

Foal's Well: NJ 0030 2988

An old water tank and spring contributing to the Grantown water supply.

Fuaran na h-Innseig: Little island spring   NH 9947 2748 Fuaranahanish Well

Gaich: The cleft   Gaeycht 1611, Gaick Roy, 1841

Lower Gaich: 1851   Nether Gaich 1771

A large farmsteading having snug dwelling house, two stories, slated with very good offices, one story, thatched and in fair state of repair. [OSNB]

Fields: Auchvallach, Loch Lands, Loch of Skaich, Duckshow. 1770

Fields: Fioch More, Auch Vattan, Coul n Doul, Lack Cat, Lack na Fual, Loin a Chroisk, Lackan Clach, Lack Vore, Rue Cannie, Druim More, Loup Vilan 1808

Mid Gaich: 1851   NJ 0152 2555   Glengynack 1901

A small farm steading dwelling house and offices, each one storey, all thatched and in fair state of repair. [OSNB] Now known as Glengynack.

Field: Tor Uachkerach 1808

Upper Gaich: 1851   NJ 0150 2578

A large farm steading comprising two dwelling houses and a number of offices, each one storey. All thatched and in middling repair. [OSNB]

Fields: Kilnfield, Longlands, Shulden, Lupvallan, Ryhillock. 1770

Fields: Peaul n Ty, Auch Vattan, Bard, Coul na Ha, Tor Uachkerach 1808

Gaich Wood: NJ 0107 2548

A large mature wood of pine and larch lying on the north side of the road from Grantown to Dulnainbridge.

Gaich Wood Cairn: NJ 0077 2538

Near the south side of this wood a short distance from Croftskellich, there is a large cairn of stones which was opened about 6 years ago and a stone chest found near to the centre, containing dust or ashes. The greater part of the cairn is taken away for the purpose of building stone fences around the adjoining fields. [OSNB]

This Bronze Age chambered cairn was thought to be lost or destroyed after the planting of trees. It survives about 100m north of Croftskellich within the mature wood.

Gaich Wood Cairn: NJ 0118 2564

Large Bronze Age cairn west of Upper Gaich in wood. Once thought to have been destroyed by tree planting, it remains an impressive structure.

Lower Gaich Wood: NJ 0174 2504

General Wade's Old Military Road   NJ 0328 2972, NJ 0277 3111

This name applies to part of the military road made under the Superintendance of General Wade, through the hills between Braemar and Fort George. The greater part of it from Spey Bridge to Bridge of Brown is still used as a country road. From Spey Bridge for a considerable distance northward it is not now traceable. [OSNB]

This road was not constructed by General Wade, but by his successor Major Caulfeild. The modern road follows its route to the Ballieward junction, where the military road heads left towards Camerory and the Dava Moor.

Glaichk n Dhian: 1809   Hollow of the fairy hill   NJ 015 294

Glaichk na Grain: 1808   NH 990 289

Glaichk na Suive: 1808   Hollow of the fox   NH 990 296

Gleann Beag: The small glen   NJ 0133 2754

A small glen extending from Craggan to Tobar Alain, situated about a mile north west of Grantown.

Glenbeg: The small glen   NJ 0078 2802   1611, Roy, 1841, Glenbeg, Half Davoch of Glenbeg 1357, 1445, 1583, Mains of Glen

Beg 1770, Glen Beg 1808

A farm steading consisting of dwelling house and office houses all

Glen Beg

Fields: Wood Toths, The Meadow, The Claggen, The Torranbeg, Burn, Meickle Ward, Mains of Glen Beg, Stocks, John McCraw's Croft, Little Fold. 1771

Fields: Dreim Vore, Shian, Dreiman Doul, Tor Flough, Ochhkan Ty More, Dreiman Shogle, Bual More, Bual a Veik, Tor Slochkcanach. 1808

Glenbeg Burn: NJ 0123 2789   Allan Burn, The Burn of Craggan 1771, Ault Glen Beg 1809, Burn of Glenbeg 1771, Another Burn of Glenbeg flows east past Glenbeg farm into Craggan Burn (Glenbeg Burn)

A large stream having its source in Tobar Alain and two head streams rising on the hills about a mile to the west of Toumnarannich at upper Glean Beag. It originally received the name of Allan Burn but owing to local usage, Glenbeg Burn is the name by which it is known in the locality. Its course being through Glean Beag- It has been written in anglicized form for similar reasons. [OSNB]

Gorton: The little cornfield or enclosure   Gortin 1583, Gorten 1611,

Easter Gorton: NJ 0170 2887   Gartonmor (Big Gorton) Roy

A farm house and out offices from one to two stories high, thatched and in good repair. [OSNB]

Fields: The Hard Ley, Bracken Riach, Barn Fold, The Land Above the Wood, Stone Fold, The Long Rigs, A cairn called the Chaple, Chaple Folds, The Short rigs, Lime Kiln Lands, The Well Croft, Sulendu, Miln Road. 1767

Fields: Corr Shellach, Brachken Rioch, Coul n Doul Vore, Crait na Ha, Prae Bard, Bual a Cloich. 1808

Wester Gorton: NJ 0098 2866   Gartonbeg (Little Gorton) Roy, Croft Gorton Beg 1808

A farmhouse and out offices from one to two stories high, thatched and in good repair. [OSNB]

Fields: The House Croft, Mid Croft, The Crooked Ridge. 1767

Fields: Suil n Duim, Touper Viel, Coul Bard, Uiten a Gorton, Stau More. 1808

Keeper's Cottage, Gorton: 1901   NJ 0100 2908

Former house of gamekeeper on Seafield estate, now used as shooting lunch hut.

Grantswell: 1841   NJ 0332 2903

Appears once in the 1841 census, but not on any map. Probably beside the well of the same name near Lynmacgregor Lots and possibly demolished when railway built.

Grants Well: NJ 0331 2903

A well below the old railway bridge on the road to Viewpoint and Achosnich.

Greengate: NJ 0315 3006   Green Gate 1809, 1812

A croft house one storey high, slated and in good repair. [OSNB]

Greengate Cottage: 1861   NJ 0325 2988   Green Gate 1871

A dwelling house one storey high, slated and in good repair. [OSNB]

Knockan Nyrap: 1808   NJ 0052 2687

Lack-n-ty vaan: Hollow of the white house   NJ 021 259

Small hollow where Inverallan fort is located.

Laggan Hill: Hill of the hollow   NJ 0038 2671   Cairn-a- Chural 1808 [OSNB]

A small heathy pasture hill, situated a short distance south west of Glenbeg farm. [OSNB] Recognisable from the radio transmitters on the summit, there's a road from Laggan to the top with good views of Strathspey and Cairngorms. On older maps known as Cairn a Chural.

Laggan Hill Cairn: NJ 0084 2681

A Bronze Age cairn with central cist on the east facing slopes of Laggan Hill.

Loch Bae: 1809   Birch tree loch   NJ 017 307

Appears on old maps, but now drained and planted with pine.

Lochend: NJ 017 254

A former settlement near Gaich.

Lochgorm: Blue green loch   NJ 0325 3132   1861

A farmhouse and out offices one storey high, the former slated, the latter thatched, in good repair. [OSNB]

Lynmacgregor Croft: Macgregor's enclosure   NJ 0285 2904 Croft McGregor 1746, Lyne Gregor Roy, Lyn McGrigor 1765, Linemacgrigor 1767, Lyne McGregor 1809 Lynemacgrigor 1841, Lynmagregor 1851, Lynmagrigor 1861, Lynemacgriger 1871, Now known as West Lynne.

Oral tradition that outlawed McGregors settled here in the 17th century, close to Castle Grant but out with old Grantown. Laird of Grant was fined for harbouring McGregors when the name was proscribed. Several of the name later lived at Lynmore, Cottertown and Camerory.

Lots of Lyne Mcgregor: NJ 0320 2925   1809, 1812

This name is applied to a number of small farms and cottages situated about one mile northwest of Grantown and about ¾ of a mile south of Castle Grant. Chiefly thatched, one storey high and in good repair. [OSNB] In 1809 there were eight lots.

Lynmacgregor Wood: NJ 033 287

Meikle Meadows: 1771   Large Meadows.   NJ 0201 2484

Adjacent to the River Spey and the lands of Gaich. Excavations for a deep channel remain visible on the southern margins. In the 19th century plans were made to cut a direct channel from the Spey for a bleach field and to power a mill, but was never completed.

Milkhillock: 1770   NH 9966 3032

Milkmoss: 1770   NH 9967 3012

Old Military Road: 1755   Old road from Grantown to Fort George.

See General Wade's Military Road

Nea Vait: 1809   NJ 017 277

Press McEwan: 1770   McEwan's copse   NJ 0137 2719   Pres ach Ewin 1808

Field: Crait-ach Ewin 1808

Quarry Cottage: see Wester Dreggie

Rafinnan: NJ 0010 2819   Roy map, Finian 1808

An old shieling on the south east face of Beinn Mhor.

Rioch: 1809   NJ 0209 2892

Rough moorland between Achosnich and Easter Dreggie, Gorton.

Rissaurie: Summer shieling   NH 991 2931   Roy, 1841, Risaury 1770, Improvement of Rysaurie 1794, Improvement of Glacknasaurie 1794, Rue Saurie 1808.

Fields: Croit, The Dell, Glachk n Suive 1808

Rinechkra: Shieling of the cattle enclosure   Rineckraw (Roy), Ryneckra 1807, Rue Nechkera 1808, Ruenechkra 1809, Rynacra 1841, Rynecra 1861

Appears in rental of 1808 linked with Finlarig farm.

Easter Ryneckra: NH 9824 3027   Easter Rynechkra 1901

A farmhouse and out offices one storey high, thatched and in good repair. [OSNB]

Fields: Crait n Taylor, Stau n Doul, Myrin Vore, Straan. 1809

Wester Ryneckra: NH 9828 3000   Wester Ryneckra 1901

Applied to two farmhouses each of which has suitable out offices, they are each one storey high, thatched and in middling repair. [OSNB]

Sgorrnadige: 1755   Peak of the dyke   Scornacheek

In 1755 when the military road was being laid down, a ditch was cut to drain Lochgorm. The ditch runs past the foot of the rock and the name was given by one of the estate factors.

Shleanaferan: Moorland   x2 NH 9997 3006, NJ 0012 2996   Sliau na Ferrin 1809, Slianfearng 1841, Sleaneferen, Sleneferen 1851, Sleabhfern 1861, Slienafairn 1901, Slianaferan

This name applies to two croft houses situated at the head of Gleann Beag. One storey high, thatched and in middling repair. [OSNB]

Site of Spey Ferry, Boat of Balliefurth to Ballintomb   NJ 0125 2452

Until around 1920, a ferryman could be summoned from Boat of Balliefurth in Abernethy to cross the River Spey to the Ballintomb side.

Tobar Alain: Clear Spring or Well of the green place, meadow. NH 9997 3099 Toperallan, Fouran Allan 1809, Fouranailean

A well emitting a quantity of water sufficient to turn the machinery of a corn mill. It is situated at the upper end of Gleann Beag and is the principal source of the Glenbeg Burn. The ancient parish name 'Inverallan' is derived from the influx of the stream issuing from it into the Spey, which originally received the name 'Allan Burn' but owing to local usage 'Glenbeg Burn' is now the name by which it is designated and known in the locality. [OSNB]

Tobar a' Choluim Chille: St Columba's Well   NJ 012 277

John Stewart, rabbit catcher, aged about 80 years old mentioned this (1914). About 100 yards above Glenbeg bridge on the right (ie the left bank of the burn) beside a stone, just beneath the steep hillside. 'It is truly a well, visibly bubbling up though feebly, and a little thread of a brooklet runs from it'.

Tom a' Chaistiel: Hillock of the castle   NH 9961 2871   Rocks called the old castle 1770, Toum Deuna Chastal 1808.

Refers to an Iron Age dun on a rocky spur of Beinn Mhor.

Tom nan Carragh: Mound of the pillars or erect stones, NJ 011 245   Tomnagarack 1771, Toum na Garroch 1808.

A small flat hill lying in the middle of Strathspey, and extending lengthwise nearly east and west for about 50 chains and about 20 in breadth. The eastern part is closely wooded and separated from the western portion by a deep trench, in sinking which about 30 years ago, human remains were found. There are 3 large standing stones on the west part of this hill, each about 8 ft high. Supposed to be the remains of Druidical circles. The name signifies, hill of the obelisks. There is also a large standing stone in the wooded part of the hill about 8 ft high. [OSNB]

Considered now a Bronze Age site c.2500BC- c.700BC. Later the hill was the assembly place for the local Regality Court and the rallying-place of the Clan Grant.

Standing Stones: NJ 0102 2457, NJ 0108 2470, NJ 0086 2516

Tordow: The black hillock   NJ 0274 3060   Roy, Tordow Tack 1765, Toredu 1770

Fields: The Black Ward 1770

Moss of Toredow: 1770   NJ 0275 3071

Tornabirag: Knoll of the point or snout   NJ 009 267   Roy, Meikle Tonabirrak 1770, Little Tornabirrack 1770, Toranabiracks, Tornabirack 1808

Tornafiach: Knoll of the raven   NJ 0302 3025   Torannafeig Roy

Torch an Uaran: 1809   The dark, dusky spring   NH 9983 3112 Dorchnuaran improvement 1773, Toich n Uaran 1809

An old shieling

Toum a Chrocher: 1809   The hangman's hill   NJ 0193 2655

Toum a Payn: 1808   NH 998 296

Toumnarannich: Hillock of the bracken slope or shieling NH 9948 3033   Toranryrannick 1794   Toum Rue Rannich 1808, Tomrannach 1841,Tomrerannach 1861, Toum of Glenbeg 1863, Tom na Rannich

A small dwellinghouse, one storey in height with offices attached, both of which are entirely roofed with sods and in wretched repair. [OSNB]

Very little survives of this croft as bulldozed for estate track. Only a few stones and a rowan tree, but bracken continues to grow in this area.

Touper Uigel: 1809   NJ 014 275

Touper Viel: 1809   NJ 0156 274

Viewpoint: NJ 0259 2913

Erected in 1914 at end of footpath leading from The Square in Grantown. Panoramic chart with names and heights of hills in view to the Cairngorms and Cromdale Hills as far as Ben Rinnes in the east and Drumochter in the south.

Viewpoint

Standing stone at Tom nan Carragh

Walks

1: Lynmacgregor, Ballieward, Camerory

From The Square walk along Seafield Avenue to the Dulaig Bridge passed the caravan site. Follow the signs for the Dava Way onto the old railway line and continue through the cutting as the path drops to the road to View Point . Rejoin the line just beyond the bridge and on the left, strung out parallel to the line are the Crofts of Lynmacgregor. Some of the original single storey houses are still inhabited with their original crofting fields extending down to the railway embankment. There were originally around a dozen lots allocated and a few were eventually demolished for larger Victorian houses and summer guests' accommodation. To the left the farm of Achnafearn appears just below the tree line and on the right across the road, through the belt of trees lies the marshy area of Polchar and the site of Old Grantown. Replaced by the new town in 1765, there were still a few stragglers living there until the 1820's.

Eventually the line crosses the main road over the impressive bridge next to the East Lodge to Castle Grant. Built by the Inverness and Perth Railway Company as a private railway halt for the Earl of Seafield, in gratitude for allowing them to build the railway through his expansive estate. The Dava Way continues gradually climbing the Ballieward Brae until it meets a track from the main road to the castle. Going to the left reaches the main road and walking back towards Grantown a short way, will reach the junction to Ballieward on the right handside. There was once an inn at Balliward which would have been a welcome sight to those climbing the brae. The single track road, sign posted Ballieward and Camerory follows the old military road from the Old Spey Bridge to Fort George. This was once the main road in and out of Strathspey from the lowlands of Nairnshire and Moray, until the current route via Huntly's Cave was created. Mail was once delivered from Aberdeen and Forres by this route.

Ballieward was a small contained crofting community, dating from the drive for agricultural improvements in the late 1770s. There were once far more croft houses than remain today. To the left are the thickly wooded Creag Bheithe Mhor and Creag Bheithe

Bheag and on the right Carn Luig. This location was one of the first plantations to be established by Sir James Grant with saplings raised on his nurseries and one of the first foresters, Alexander McGregor lived at Camerory. At Upper Camerory the surfaced road stops at a gate and the continuing track is all that remains of the original military road. From here there are great views to Ben Rinnes stretching west along the Cromdale Hills. The track skirts the plantation fence to the watershed overlooking the Dava Moor and beyond. From here it's possible to continue crossing the Dava via Anaboard or following the fence round Carn Luig to join the main road or a little further on, re-join the Dava Way back to Grantown.

2: Viewpoint, Achosnich, Gorton and Dreggie

Starting from The Square follow the signs to Viewpoint along Seafield Avenue. From the Dulaig water fall the route is well signed from the railway line and uphill through the hazelnut wood. The initial climb is short and steep but there is a bench to sit on and take in the view over Grantown, nestling in the sylvan hollow and the Cromdale Hills. The walk continues through birch woods until the farm road to Achosnich is reached. The Viewpoint chart is on the right among a few pine trees. It's possible to return to Grantown the same way or down by the farm road to re-join the Dava Way along the disused railway line or by the main road.

For those who wish to continue further, follow the farm road to Achosnich and through the farm steading and passed the cottage to the rear. The track leads to a hill gate with a deer fence and stile. It's easier walking to stay out with the fence as the ground inside is heavily rutted with recent tree planting. Follow the fence up towards Gorton Hill. Another gate and stile gives access now to another track passed some ruins and a solitary tree to the cairn.

Here on a fine day are commanding views from Ben Rinnes, Cromdale Hills, Cairngorms and round to Meall Cuach in Drumochter. Continue down to the Keeper's Cottage in Glen Beg, where a gate and track lead back to the bridge at Dulaig.

Start at either the car park by Old Inverallan cemetery and walk the single track road to join the main road at Kirkton, or on the old road by Kirkton Cottage, where there is limited parking.

Follow the sign for Glen Beg and begin walking with the Glen Beg Burn on the left and up and under the old railway bridge. This follows the old church road that went from upper Glen Beg to the original Inverallan church. The road originally was more direct from where it crosses the mainroad. It then carried on to the right of Toum a Chrocher (hill of the hangman) and rejoined the current road near the modern houses. The field on the left beyond the bridge was known as Croft Miller and would have belonged to the miller at Craggan. Beside the fields of Croft Farquhar the road forks, either continue on towards Glenbeg farm or take the track on the right towards Gorton. The former crosses the Glenbeg burn and rises to the farm, leaving the wooded glen behind and opening out onto the moor of Laggan and Bheinn Mhor. Behind the farm, tracks can be followed to explore the burial cairn or climb to the trig point on Bheinn Mhor.

Otherwise continue up the glen and the track swings round by a ford, over the Glen Beg burn and passing Wester Gorton. Beyond here a track veers left uphill towards the Keeper's Cottage and Gorton Hill. Going through a gate in the deer fence the track levels off all the way to the head of the glen. It's possible to follow the estate roads all the way to the Rynechra (shieling of the cattle pen) which can be seen in the distance. Though remote, it was a well chosen spot as the sun always seems to shine on its fields.

A solitary larch tree, tilting from the wind and a gable end is all that's left of Sleanafearn and a red corrugated iron roof marks the Foal's well. This was one of many springs that were used early in the 20th century to pipe water to Grantown. Its demands grew, especially during the summer when the population rose dramatically with visitors. For the return journey follow the track past Gorton to Wester Dreggie and down to Grantown. On a good day rewarded with fine views over the town, Cairngorms and Cromdale Hills or alternatively take the track back to the fork above Croft Farquhar.

Starting at Rôches Moutonnées lay by, walk to the road leading up to Easter Laggan. On the fringes of the wood and in the field to the right are outlines of former cottages, once occupied by the labourers at the limestone quarries on Laggan Hill. Just before the entrance to Easter Laggan, go through a gate on the right and follow the track marked for Laggan Hill and the transmitter pylon. A short climb to the top is rewarded with views over Strathspey. It's possible to continue along the watershed to Beinn Mhor or visit the limestone quarries and cup marked stones to the south west on Laggan Hill. Other archaeological remains are to the south east: two cairns in Gaich Wood and one on the moor. Return by the road to Laggan.

Cross the main road to Ballintomb farm and ask permission to access the standing stones at Tom nan Carragh. Often there are sheep with lambs or crops around the site. It's easiest to walk along the old railway line or alternatively walk along the banks of the Spey from Inverallan passed Tarrig Mhore and the Meikle Meadows. This site is of great antiquity and the location must have held some significance. It's been a ceremonial meeting place since the standing stones were erected to monitor the sun and moon and much later clan Grant, the Regality Court and Figgat Fair all gathered here at one time. A ferry also crossed the Spey near here until the 1920's from Boat of Balliefurth.

Achosnich

Bronze Age Burial Cist, Laggan Hill

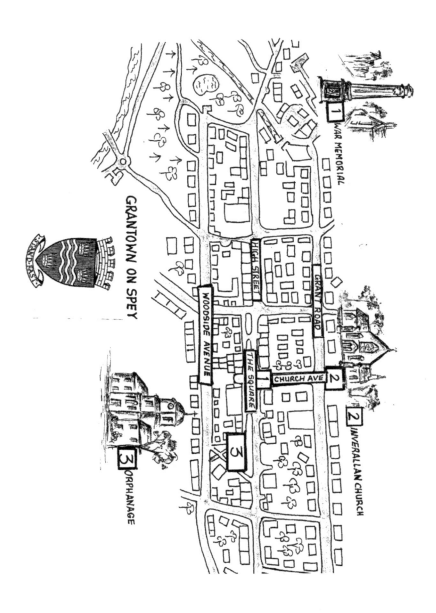

CHAPTER 3

GRANTOWN ON SPEY

WAR MEMORIAL 1

INVERALLAN CHURCH 2

ORPHANAGE 3

HIGH STREET

GRANT ROAD

WOODSIDE AVENUE

THE SQUARE

CHURCH AVE

Grantown-on-Spey, Inverallan, Anagach to Craigroy

Anagach: The dangerous ford. Annagaugh 1771, Anagach Lots 1-5 1841.

The name applies to a few cot houses situated near to Spey Bridge on the west side of the River Spey. They are one storey high, slated and in good repair. [OSNB]

Before Spey Bridge was built there were three fords lower down. One was in the form of a zigzag and could be crossed only when the water was at its lowest.

Mid Anagach: NJ 0452 2674

Easter Anagach: NJ 0479 2694 East Anagach 1841

Wester Anagach: NJ 0433 2659 West Anagach 1841

Back of Anagach: NJ 0518 2741

Anagach Moss: NJ 0415 2766 Moss of Annagauch 1768

A small area of moor situated to the north of Anagach Wood. [OSNB]

Anagach Wood: NJ 0380 2740 Plantation of Anagauch 1771

Loch Anagach: NJ 0360 2683 Roy, Loch of Annagauch 1771

Now drained and planted.

Bell Hillock: NJ 0267 2612

Beside Inverallan churchyard. Probable site for ringing church bell for old Inverallan church.

Black Park (The): 1813 NJ 0373 2806 Seafield Park, Grantown Park

Recreational area gifted to the inhabitants of Grantown by the Seafield estate. Former site of Strathspey Farmers Club show.

Burn of Grantown: NJ 0347 2803

Diverted to flow down Burnfield, for bleaching field and flax industry. Also first water supply for inhabitants.

Craigroy: 1851 Red craig NJ 0561 2726

This name applied to a small crofthouse, with outhouses, all one storey high, thatched and in middling condition. [OSNB]

Craigroy Wood: NJ 061 274

Crow Wood: NJ 0632 2881

Free Church Wood: NJ 0318 2715

Upper Faevoit: 1768   Submerged or drowned bog   NJ 0375 2844   Clover Park 1778

The marsh was situated beside the hospital before it was drained and the stream flowed through Heathfield.

Nether Faevoit: 1768   Lower submerged or drowned bog   NJ 0392 2820

Area across from Heathfield, bordering on sports centre and golf course.

General Wade's Military Road: NJ 0349 2726

Part of the military road made under the Superintendance of General Wade through the hills between Braemar amd Fort George. The greater part of it from Spey Bridge to Bridge of Brown is still used as a country road. From Spey Bridge for a considerable distance northward it is not now traceable. [OSNB]

This often repeated account is wrong. The road was built in 1754 to the River Spey at Old Spey Bridge, under the supervision of Major William Caulfeild.Building work probably began on the northern section later that year or in 1755.

Grantown: NJ 0335 2797   Baile nan Granndach, Baile Urr, New Grantown 1768 [OSNB]

Founded by Sir James Grant on the moor of Faevoit in 1765.

Grantown-on-Spey:

The council added the title Grantown–on-Spey in 1898, when the town became a Police Burgh.

Back Street: NJ 0355 2794   South Street

Baptists Chapel: NJ 0310 2765

A small chapel, slated and in very good condition. Number of sittings 380. Number of communicants at the last dispensation of the sacrament 253. Property of the Baptist Community of Grantown.

Completed in 1851, its best remembered preacher was local man, Peter Grant, whose collection of Gaelic hymns is world famous.

Bathing Pool: NJ 0289 2660

A sandy bank on the Spey, beside road to Inverallan cemetery. Popular spot in summer for swimming.

Beachan Court: NJ 0267 2785

Birchview Terrace: NJ 0318 2785

Black Bull Hotel: NJ 0326 2780

A two storey house with offices, slated and in excellent condition. There is a public house directly opposite to the hotel. [OSNB]

Bleechfield: 1768 NJ 0348 2799

Where bleeching in the production of linen from flax was carried out.

Braemoray Avenue: NJ 0278 2730

Breweree Park: 1768 NJ 0353 2775

Burnfield Avenue: NJ 0349 2799

Water for Grantown's first industries came from the burn which ran through this field. It was also used as a bleach field for linen made from locally grown flax.

Cairngorm Avenue: NJ 0262 2765

Caledonian Bank: NJ 0325 2784

A large two storey house, slated and in excellent condition. This is the banker's residence. Part of this building is the North British and Mercantile Insurance Office. [OSNB]

Castle Road: NJ 0348 2815

This led directly to Old Grantown and Castle Grant.

Castle Road East: NJ 0354 2830

Chapel Court: NJ 0308 2772

Chapel Road: NJ 0309 2767

Church: (Chapel of Ease) NJ 0320 2803 Inverallan Church

This church, a stone erection, slated and in excellent condition, is situated immediately west of The Square in the village of Grantown. Its southern end is surmounted by a bell. Erected by the Heritors for the accommodation of the people living in the neighbourhood of Grantown-The Parish church proper, being situate too far distant for convenience. [OSNB]

This was later replaced on the same site by the current Inverallan Church in 1886.

Church Avenue: NJ 0324 2801

Leads from The Square to Inverallan Church, the Seafield Memorial Church, consecrated in 1886.

Coppice Court: NJ 0296 2785

Coppice Lane: NJ 0295 2790

Court House: NJ 0342 2802

A fine stone building in course of erection in 'The Square' of the village of Grantown, opposite Lethendry Cottage, which has been erected for the purpose of holding small Debt Court by the Sheriffs of Elgin and Inverness-shires. It contains police cells and accommodation for the person who takes charge of it. [OSNB]

It was completed in 1868 shortly after the Ordnance Survey Place Name Book was compiled.

Curling Ponds: NJ 036 275

Dulaig Court: NJ 0277 2784

Dunbar's Hotel: NJ 0316 2765 Strathspey Hotel

This hotel, which is also a posting establishment, is a two storey house slated and in very good condition. It has office houses attached which are one storey high and in good condition. [OSNB]

Dunstaffanage Brae: NJ 0300 2728

East End: NJ 0348 2813

This name is applied to the small street in the village of Grantown which lies north east of The Square. The houses in this part of the village are principally one storey high, slated and in good condition. [OSNB]

Female School: NJ 0352 2800 Grantown Museum

A neat substantial house, slated and in excellent condition. The school and schoolmistress residence are under the same roof. Daily average number of scholars 100. This school is in connexion with the Established Church and receives an endowment of £16 per Annum from a bequest out of which the school was erected. [OSNB]

The former school building now houses Grantown Museum.

Forest Road: NJ 0341 2771

Free Church: NJ 0324 2747

A very substantial stone building slated and in excellent condition. It is situated quite near to the manse. Its western end is surmounted by a bell. No of sittings 600. [OSNB]

Free Church School: NJ 0295 2743

A one storey stone building situated at the southern end of the village of Grantown. The average number of scholars attending this school is 120. It is supported by the Free Church congregation of Grantown. [OSNB]

Garth Hotel: NJ 0343 2809The oldest part was built in 1769 by James Grant, the clerk to Sir James Grant. In 1776 it became a textile factory. Since then a hotel and war time officers' mess.

Gas Works: NJ 0353 2777

These works consist of a small gasometer and two small stone buildings, the whole enclosed by a fence. They are situated near the parish school. [OSNB]

Golf Course Road: NJ 0368 2799

Grant Arms Hotel: NJ 0338 279

This hotel is a two storey house slated and in very good condition. The office houses in connexion with this building are wood (Aug 1867) in the course of erection. [OSNB]

The current building dates from 1875, and largely replaced the older building, visited anonymously by Queen Victoria in 1860.

Grant Park: NJ 0296 2706   Curling Pond, Skating Pond

Popular venue for winter sports. Curling bonspiels held here by the Strathspey Curling Club, formed in 1856.

Grant Road: NJ 0294 2763

Grantown Station: NJ 0244 2697   Grantown-on-Spey West

This station, situated 48 miles by rail from Inverness, consists of offices for passengers and luggage traffic, waiting rooms for passengers, a double platform. The station agent's house and three small cottages for the accommodation of porters are situated quite near to the station. Everything about the station is in good repair. [OSNB]

Opened in 1863, it closed on 18 Oct 1965. The station master's house survives, but the station was bulldozed in the early 1980's.

Heathfield Road: NJ 0364 2817

High Street: NJ 0320 2773

This name is applied to that part of the main street of Grantown which lies between Dunbar's Hotel and the southern end of The Square. All the houses in this street, with one exception, are slated and in very good condition. [OSNB]

Ian Charles Cottage Hospital: 1885   NJ 0354 2850

The land and funding for the hospital was granted by Caroline, Dowager Countess of Seafield in memory of her only son Ian Charles, 8th Earl of Seafield, who died young. Opened 1885.

Inverallan: Mouth of the Allan Burn   NJ 0254 2592

The confluence of the Allan or Glenbeg burn with the Spey. Name was subsequently given to the surrounding lands, church and parish.

Barony of Inverallan: 1611

Inverallan Cemetery: NJ 0269 2603

Inverallan Court: NJ 0320 2795

Inverallan Church (Old):   NJ 0266 2603   Kirk of Inverellan Roy

Site in Inverallan cemetery of the old church of Inverallan since the union of the Parishes of Cromdale, Inverallan and Advie. [OSNB] Situated close to the wall with the Pictish stone.

Inverallan Fort: NJ 0259 2606

Inverallan House: 1901   NJ 0259 2606

A good dwelling house with ornamental ground and outhouses attached. Occupied by Mr Smith, Factor to the Earl of Seafield. The proprietor. [OSNB]

Inverallan Pictish Stone: NJ 0254 2601

A Class 1 Pictish symbol stone in Inverallan cemetery.

Milne of Inverallem: 1611

Kirkton: NJ 0260 2612   1841, Kirktown of Inverallan 1770

Fields: Bell Hillock, Lynmore, Touper Hillock, Touper Feadock (Figgat), Millars Haugh, Blackhills. 1770

Lower Kirktown 1851, Kirktown of Inverallan 1770, Kirktoun of Kylentra 1771,

Upper Kirktown 1851   NJ 0221 2645

Fields: Lagganriach, The Kiln How, The Blue How, Linmore. 1770

Killindraw: 1851   Wooded Valley   NJ 0281 2761 Roy Coildraw, Farm of Kylentra 1770, Killintraw 1861.

Kylintra Burn: NJ 0287 2684   The Burn of Kylentra 1771

A small burn which rises to the west of Grantown. Its general course is south east passing the lower end of Grantown and flows into the Spey at Kylintra. [OSNB] Above the old Highland Railway line it is called 'Corshelloch Burn'.

Kylintra Crescent: NJ 0278 2761

Kylintra Sawmill: 1901   NJ 0288 2672

Three sheds attached to one another which form a saw mill, a dwelling house with a shed attached for an office house. The whole are one story high and in good condition. [OSNB]

Moor of Kylentraw: 1770   NJ 0291 2814   Moss of Kylentraw 1768 (Mossie), Meadow of Kylentra 1768

Kylintra Wood: NJ 0277 2690

Lady Garden Wood: NJ 0355 2703

Named after the sister of Sir James Grant, the founder of Grantown.

Lag nan Caorach: Sheep hollow. NJ 0460 2794

A hollow in Anagach Woods, the whole extent of which is a moss situated about a mile south east of Grantown square. [OSNB]

Lethendry Cottage: NJ 0337 2803

A handsome two storey dwelling house with office houses in its rear, slated and in excellent condition. This name has recently been applied to this cottage. [OSNB]

Loch nan Geadas: Loch of the pike   NJ 0503 2817

A swampy area situated in Lag nan Caorach. [OSNB]

Lochnageds Burn: 1802   NJ 0511 2844

Mackay Avenue: NJ 0289 2773

Named after Dick Mackay a former Provost of Grantown.

Manse (Free Church):   NJ 0322 2746

A two storey dwelling house situated close to the Free Church. It is built of stone, slated and in excellent condition. Property of the Free Church Body of Grantown. [OSNB]

Manse (Baptist):   NJ 3030 8276

A very handsome cottage, one storey high, slated and in excellent condition. It is situated immediately behind the Baptist Chapel from which it is separated by the garden attached to the manse. [OSNB]

Market Road: NJ 0353 2809

Market Stance: NJ 0370 2803

This is the first field north of Back Street. There is a wooden house situated in the middle of it. The whole field is enclosed by a paling. There is a monthly market held here for cattle only and a half yearly market for the hiring of servants and is a chartered market. [OSNB]

McGregor Avenue: NJ 0268 2759

Named after William McGregor a saddler and former Provost of Grantown.

Mineral Well: NJ 0304 2824

Miss Grant's Garden: Miss Grant's Park 1771

Named after the sister of Sir James Grant, the founder of Grantown.

Moss of Grantown: The Mossie   NJ 0323 2836

Mossie Road: NJ 0333 2820

Road lead to the local peat moss.

Ms Grant's Park: 1768   NJ 0343 2735

National Bank of Scotland: NJ 0335 2801   Morlich House

A very neat two storey dwelling house slated and in excellent condition. There is one small outhouse in connexion with this building. [OSNB]

Pleasure Walk: 1771

From the garden of Lady Grant, the sister of Sir James Grant.

Poorhouse: 1851   NJ 0464 2836   Cromdale Poor House
1861, Parish Cottages

A long cottage, one storey high, thatched and in good repair. Built for the lodgings of the Poor of the Parish. Property of the Parochial Board. [OSNB] Closed in the 1960s and replaced with Grant House.

Poorhouse Wood: NJ 0457 2842

Port Wood: NJ 0579 2826

Post Office: NJ 0323 2782

A neat stone house slated and in good condition. This is a money order office. There are 3 arrivals at and 3 dispatches from this office of mails, daily. [OSNB]

Priest's Stone: NJ 0267 2600

A standing stone in Inverallan cemetery, inscribed with a Latin cross on both sides. Reputed burial place of St Figgat.

Revoan Drive: Slope or shieling of the bothy   NJ 0258 2780

A former farm and bothy in the Cairngorms and name of villa in Seafield Avenue.

Rhuardan Court: NJ 0284 2801

River Spey   Hawthorn river   NJ 032 267   Uisge Spe, Spey River   1771 [OSNB]

Royal Bank of Scotland: NJ 0315 2768

This is a large two storey house, with offices and garden attached. This house is the residence of the banker. [OSNB]   Opened in 1864 and due for closure in 2018.

School: NJ 0349 2780   Grantown Grammar School, Grantown Primary School

A stone building at the eastern side of Grantown. It is slated and in excellent condition. Average number of scholars in attendance about 200. It is supported by voluntary contributions. There is a small belfry in this building. This school is not a parish school although it is sometimes so termed in the locality. It was erected by the Earl of Seafield as a Grammar School for the neighbourhood of Grantown, but it is not now exclusively used for that purpose, as the ordinary branches are taught. [OSNB]

Until the 1960s this was Grantown Grammar School. The oldest parts of the building date from 1836.

Seafield Avenue: NJ 0296 2806

Seafield Court: NJ 0306 2807

Seafield Estate Offices: NJ 0332 2797   The Cairngorms National Park Headquarters

Shankland Court: NJ 02940 2758

Named after Sir Thomas Shankland, a former Provost of Grantown.

South Street: NJ 0351 2790

A row of one storey cottages all slated and in very good condition. This row of houses is parallel to the main street of Grantown and east of that part of it called The Square. [OSNB]

South West High Street: NJ 0299 2751

Speybridge: NJ 0388 2664   Lots of Spey Bridge 1851, 1861

This name is applied to some small farm houses lying between the village of Grantown and the bridge which crosses the Spey. They are all close to the main road. [OSNB]

Spey Bridge: (Old Spey Bridge)   NJ 0397 2633

A stone built bridge, which crosses the River Spey, about a mile south east of Grantown and about a quarter of a mile north west of Grantown Railway Station. It was built in the year 1754 by the 33rd Regiment, under the superintendence of Lord Charles Hay, Colonel. It is now greatly out of repair and considered unsafe for heavy loads. A County Bridge. [OSNB]

New Spey Bridge: NJ 0337 2681

Constructed of concrete and designed by the engineering firm, Blyth and Blyth. It was opened by the Mackintosh of Mackintosh on 11 Dec 1931.

Spey Avenue: NJ 0332 2745

Speyside Orphan Hospital: The Speyside Charity School NJ 0336 2791

On the south side of the Square (in the village of Grantown) stands the Speyside Orphan Hospital, built on a neat design in 1824. There are at present about 30 children in the hospital, boys and girls. None are admitted under seven or continued above 14 years of age. According to the deed of settlement, the children admitted must be natives of either of the parishes of Cromdale, Abernethy, Duthil, Inveraven or Knockando. All the children are supplied with clothing, board and education. 'New Stat Acc' [Statistical Account] [OSNB]

The clock tower was largely financed from an unusual local collection for 'Russian Sufferers' of the Napoleonic Wars.

[The] Square: NJ 0334 2793

The name is applied to that portion of the village of Grantown in which the Grant Arms Hotel and the National Bank of Scotland are situated. It lies directly between the East End and the West End. The houses in it are partly two and partly one storey high, all slated and in good condition. [OSNB]

Originally the new town's market place, most of the first houses were built here. The oldest surviving two, built in 1768, stand in the north east corner adjacent to the Court House.

St Figgat's Well: NJ 0283 2648   Touper Feadock 1770

A spring reputed to be associated with St Figgat, the early Christian missionary for the Inverallan area. Site was maintained in the early 20th cent, but has subsequently become overgrown.

Station Wood: NJ 0253 2688

Strathspey: NH 8848 1175, NJ 2880 4497 [OSNB]

Traditionally the country on both sides of the River Spey, between the two Craigellachies.

Strathspey Drive: NJ 0261 2743

Strathspey Gardens: NJ 0341 2789

Strathspey Road: NJ 0265 2754

Target (The):   NJ 032 286

A former rifle range.

West End: NJ 0303 2749

This name is applied to that portion of Grantown which lies south west of High St. The houses in it are nearly all one storey high, slated and in good condition. [OSNB]

Woodburn Crescent: NJ 0290 2746

Woodburn Drive: NJ 0277 2747

Woodburn Place: NJ 0283 2749

Woodlands Terrace: NJ 0271 2720   Station Road

Linked the town with Grantown West railway station, when the main London-Inverness line reached Grantown in 1863.

Wood Park: NJ 0318 2737

Woodside Avenue: NJ 0323 2750

A number of Victorian villas built for summer lets.

Woodside Court: NJ 0336 2774

The Speyside Orphanage

Walks

Start in The Square, the historic centre of Grantown, which was founded in 1765 by Sir James Grant. The first house of the new town was built on the north side of The Square for James Grant a weaver from Rothiemurchus. Sadly the house has not survived, as it was demolished in the 1850's, to be replaced by the National Bank of Scotland, now called Morlich House. The south side is dominated by the Grant Arms Hotel, though not the building that Queen Victoria visited incognito in 1860. Beside it Speyside House, a former orphanage and the only A listed building in Strathspey and Badenoch. This fine Georgian building was home to orphaned children, mostly from the surrounding parishes until it closed in 1975. The art deco building a few doors further down was the cinema which closed in the 1970's and now houses the British Legion.

In the centre of The Square the war memorial is a simple column of grey granite on a pedestal with bronze wreath and panel of a highland infantryman. Two hundred and fifty two men and women are listed, who were born or resided in the district, who had enlisted in Strathspey, or had former family connections with the locality. It was unveiled by the Countess of Seafield in 1921. Leaving the Square walk down the High St with its varied independent shops, former post office, banks, Baptist Chapel and Victorian Institute (1897). Sadly there are also several empty properties on both sides of the street.

At the turn of the 19th century when the town had grown way beyond Sir James Grant's expectations, it could boast a population of 1500 plus branches of the Caledonian, National and Royal Banks, the Strathspey National Security Savings Bank, several hotels, a court house, public hall, public water supply, a gas works, an orphanage (1824), cottage hospital (1884), curling and cyclist clubs, Freemasons, public library (1859), agricultural society (1812) a golf course (1890) and two railway stations. By the 1950's Grantown had 15 hotels and over 40 good quality shops

At the west end of the High Street by the Silver Bridge a foot path to the left leads through Grant Park and along the banks of the Kylentra Burn, passed a pond once popular with skaters and curlers to end at the by-pass road. Cross the road and follow the single track road upstream beside the River Spey. The road ends at a small car park used by fishermen at Old Inverallan Cemetery. Here's the site of the earliest ecclesiastical origins of the parish. A single standing stone with incised Christian crosses perhaps marks the resting place of the elusive early St Figgat, who preached in the area and to whom a well is also dedicated near-by. A Pictish Class 1 stone is embedded in the cemetery wall close to the site of the original church of which nothing remains. An early baptismal font also rests by the tree at the entrance gate. Just beyond the cemetery, the path crosses a bridge over the Glen Beg burn where it flows into the Spey. This confluence is Inverallan or the mouth of the Allan Burn, to use its older name and the origin for the parish name.

Return to the road and follow it back to the main road and the pavement that heads towards the new Spey Bridge. Opened in 1931, its single span was built with concrete and replaced the older bridge which could no longer support vehicular traffic. From the roundabout at the bridge return to Grantown by Spey Avenue or a little beyond it, the Old Military Road through the woods.

2: The Square, Anagach Wood, Poorhouse Wood

Starting again in The Square walk down Forest Road past the fire station and old telephone exchange and cross the road to continue towards Anagach Woods. On the left a sign marks the Speyside Way and numerous other walks of various distances within the woodland. The direct route following the Speyside Way will eventually lead to Cromdale Church, passing the curling ponds, Anagach Moss, golf course (1890) and Lag nan Caorach (hollow of the sheep). Way markers to Poorhouse Wood take the path close to the former site of a single story extended house which was still in use in the 1960s for homeless, poor people. Now demolished it's still possible to see remains of the foundations. A path from here leads back to the golf course and a short walk across the course to Golf Course Road and Market Road.

The Market Stance and Black Park on the right were donated

to the town by the Seafield family for public use. Here markets were held, sporting events, agricultural shows and Highland Games. Crossing the junction of Heathfield Road and South Street (Back Street) leads to Market Road, once a sea of animals coming and going to market and the noise of the smiddy which was also located here. Markets were removed from The Square in 1852. Where Market Road joins Castle Road, turn left. Castle Road has many listed buildings and the distinctive Garth Hotel (1769) which was home to a previous clerk to Sir James Grant and also housed Grantown's first industrial textile factory. The road branching to the left called Burnfield, is named after a burn diverted to flow down here, not only for the public water supply, but was also used in linen manufacturing. The green on either side, which is now a large car park was once used for drying flax. Grantown Museum located in Burnfield, a former girl's school, is worth a visit. It tells the history of the town, has a small archive and hosts various exhibitions.

The imposing building on the corner of The Square is the Court House. Opened in 1868, it housed the police station, jail and meeting rooms for the provost and burgh council. Grantown was elevated to Police Burgh status in 1898 and gloried in the new title of Grantown-on-Spey. To the right of the war memorial the former Seafield Estate Office block (1884) now accomodates The Cairngorms National Park H.Q. Beyond the war memorial the avenue of trees to the right lead to Inverallan Church or the Seafield Memorial Church of Inverallan. The current building was opened in 1886 by Caroline Dowager Countess of Seafield in memory of her late husband, the 7th Earl of Seafield and only young son, Ian Charles 8th Earl of Seafield. She also erected the Ian Charles Hospital in 1885 in memory of her son, which has admirably served the community, though its closure is now imminent.

3: The Square, Old Spey Bridge to Craigroy

The final walk from the Square goes down Forest Road and continues along the Old Military Road to join the road beside the Spey. The Old Military Road is often mistaken for a Wade road, but it was built by Major Caulfeild, his successor in Scotland. Stretching from Blairgowrie to Braemar and over the Lecht to the Old Spey Bridge, it continues onto Fort George on the Moray Firth. The road and bridge were instrumental in Sir James Grant's decision to establish Grantown where he did. Turn left on reaching the road and walk past the row of houses and villas known as Speybridge.

Beyond where the road curves, leads across the old bridge. On the far side, which is in the parish of Abernethy, a marker stone rests beside the bridge, erected by the soldiers to commemorate the completion of the road to the Spey. Walk back to the sign to Anagach on the right and follow the track past the farms of Wester, Mid and Easter Anagach. Before the bridge was built there had once been a ford here and also a Loch Anagach which was later drained and planted. The track eventually reaches Craigroy where the choice is to turn left following a trail into the wood that joins the Speyside Way or right and return to the old bridge by the banks of the river.

Hogmanay 2017 in The Square

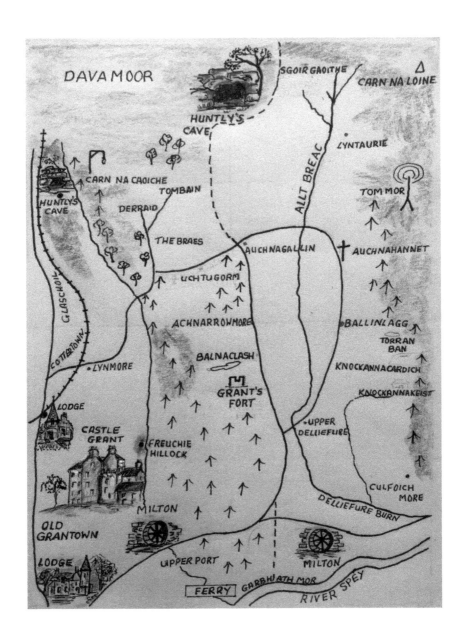

CHAPTER 4

Castle Grant, The Braes, Auchnagallin to Port

Davochs 1773
Davoch of Castle Grant

Dunan, Clashndunan, Den of Clashndunan, Old Grantown, Lynmore, Achnafearn, Lynmagrigor, Cottartown of Castle Grant, Upper Feavoit improvement, Nether Feavoit improvement, Rynaceardich improvement, Shianaittin improvement, Ryhuine improvement, Wester Lymnkilns, Easter Lymkilns, Aittendow improvement, Ainabord improvement, Camrory improvement, Improvement above Belliward,

Davoch of Achnahannet

Knockannakeardich, Ballinluig, Achnahannet, Wester Achnagaln, Easter Achnagaln, Derrilean improvement, Lynsaurie improvement, Little Lynsaurie improvement, Altarsin improvement, Badchaor improvement.

Davoch of Achnarrowmore

Achnarrowmore, Auchtobeg, Park at Gartkeen, Balnaclash, Croftnloan

Davoch of Achnarrowbegg

Tombain, Achtogorm, Achnarrowbegg, Croft of Craigbegg, Craigbegg, Culquoichbegg, Kichanroy improvement, Park of Derraid.

Davoch of Dellafour

Knockannakiest, Easter Dellafoure, Wester Dellafoure, Corn and Miln Croft of Dellefure, Upper Dellifoure, Shianmore and Mein improvements.

Davoch of Port

Milntown of Castle Grant and miln, Anagach, Wester Port, Upper Port, Mid Port. Easter Port, Boat Croft of Cromdale, Raitt and Feaglass improvement, Rychraggan improvement, Lagnacaorach improvement.

Allt a'Bhacain: Stream of the knoll   NJ 0462 2994

A small burn rising between Creag Bheithe Bheag and Creag Bheithe Mhor at Camerory and flowing east through the grounds at Castle Grant, and into Allt an Fhitich below Castle Grant. [OSNB]

Allt an Fhithich: The raven burn   NJ 0473 2992   Burn of Ault-Niech 1770, Altnich Burn 1802, Ault Neich1805

A large burn rising due south of Carn Clais an Eich, flowing under Creag an Fhithich and onwards until it joins the River Spey south of the Boat of Cromdale. [OSNB]

Allt Breac: The dappled or spotted burn   NJ 0617 3261

A burn rising at Uaigh Mhor flowing south easterly for a distance of about 4 miles and ultimately falls into the Spey east of Cromdale. [OSNB]

Altguarch: Appears in 1851 census.

Easter Auchnagallin: 1851   Field of the rock or field of the stranger NJ 0515 3385   Auchnagall 1611. Easter Achnagaln 1767, Easter Achnagaul 1802, Easter Achnagallin 1861

A steading and dwelling house, one storey high, thatched and in middling repair. [OSNB]

Fields: Fae Shallach, Small Fold, Dears Croft, How of the Torbuie, Lauchen, Calfs Ward, Lands of TomnaCairn, Lagmore, Achna Cuach, Torran Buie, Belna Foilack, Laggan Goun. 1802

Mid Auchnagallin: NJ 0523 3374

A farm steading and dwelling house, one storey high, thatched and in good repair. [OSNB]

Wester Auchnagallin: NJ 0503 3336   Auchnagaul1611, Wester Auchnygaull 1767, Achnygaull 1767, Wester Achnagaul 1802, Wester Achnagallin 1861,

A farm steading and dwelling houses, one storey high, thatched and in good repair. [OSNB]

Fields: Blue croft, Cards How, Calf Ward, Black Field, Due Hallow, Feamore. 1802

Auchnahannet: Field of the chapel NJ 0593 3337 Auchnahandatt 1611, Auchnahanit, Achnahannet 1767, 1901

A farm steading and dwelling house, one storey high, thatched and in good repair. [OSNB]

Fields: The Strype of the Clash, Feamore, Kiln Croft, Fea Lochan, Guillechen More, Gooss How, Meikle Fold 1802

Fields: Gailich n More, Coul n Leish, Crait na ha, Crait Cruin. 1810

Auchnahannet Chapel: NJ 0618 3310

Nothing is known about the early history of this Christian site. A field name on Ballinlag farm adjoining Auchnahannet is Auch n Chupple 1810, Field of the chapel.

Knock of Auchnahannnet: Hillock of the chapel field   NJ 0604 3381   Knock of Achnahannet 1767, Knock of Achnahanit 1851

A farm steading and dwelling house, one storey high, thatched and in good repair. [OSNB]

Fields: The Bog, Black Shean, Reinachule, Dogs How, Little Croft, Stony Croft, North Brae, The Haugh. 1802

Upper Auchnahannet: NJ 0622 3385

Auchnarrowbeg: Small corn field   NJ 0384 3286   Litill Auchnarrowe 1611, Auchnarrowbegg 1767, Auchenarrow Beg (Lag) 1810, Auchinarrowbeg 1851

Field: Barnfield 1802

Fields: Staun Leish, Lack Vore, Stau Cairn Cloigh, Coul n Tye, Stau na Criu Curan 1810

Auchnarrow School: NJ 0490 3253   Achnarrow School House 1901

Auchnarrowmore: Large corn field   NJ 05003 32280   Meikle Auchnarrowe 1611, Auchnarrowmore 1767, Achnarrow 1861, 1901

A farm dwelling house, steading and offices, one storey high, partly slated and partly thatched, in good condition. [OSNB]

Fields: Beul More, Auch na Cairn, Coul na Ha, Braichn Criu, Piroich More, Dallu Fat, Blaa More, Bard na Laogh, Tau Cuchan, Lachk na Baunnock, Touper Fy 1810

Bail a'Chaisteil: Castle town   NJ 0376 2949

The old name for Castle Grant, used in charters until 1694, when the area granted the Regality of Grant. From then known as Castle

Grant after the clan.

Bail na Granndach: Farmstead of Grant NJ 0376 2949 Grantown Roy , Old Grantown 1809, Old Grantown Park 1809, Lands of Old Grantown 1812

Replaced by the current town in 1765, and reports state old village was finally abandoned by 1823.

Ballieward Belts: NJ 0345 3054

Ballinlagg: Farmstead of the hollow NJ 0638 3286 Ball n Luig 1767, Bellenluig 1802

This place consists of a farmhouse, steading and offices, one storey high in fair condition. [OSNB]

Fields: Kiln Hillock, Chapel Field, Read Braes, South Braes, Lands of Touperendonich. 1802

Fields: Torran Yeorn, Lack na Putich, Auch n Chupple, Auch na Criach, Knockan Doul. 1810

Balnaclash: Farmstead of the ravine NJ 0555 3189 1812, 1815

A farmhouse and offices one storey, former slated, the latter thatched, all in fair condition. [OSNB]

Fields: Bual a Du, Lachk na Baunnock, Tau Cuchan, Bard na Laogh, Crait n Lone. 1810

Balnaclash Wood: NJ 0552 3223

Blar Mor: Large moss NJ 0607 3246

A large area of moorland where the people of the district used to cut their peat, situated on the west side of Allt Breac, north of Delliefure. [OSNB]

Blaremore: A school NJ 0632 3197

This is a small school with the exception of a small grant from government, it is supported by the farmers in the district. It does not belong to any denomination. [OSNB]

There was also a Poor House in the vicinity NJ 0637 3178

Boat of Cromdale: NJ 0663 2915 Boat Croft Roy, Boat Croft 1771, 1802

This name applies to the house occupied by the ferryman at Boat of Cromdale, part of which is used as a public house. There is a small farm and out offices attached, one storey high, thatched and in good repair. There is also a public ferry across the River Spey at this place for the conveyance of passengers, horses and cattle. [OSNB]

Fields: The Little Moss, Lands of Tombuie, The Banks, Steep Braes 1771

Boathouse Wood: NJ 0656 2909

Broom Hill: NJ 026 327

Broom Hillock: NJ 047 303

Braes of Castle Grant: NJ 033 330

Area of south facing high ground above Allt an Fhithich, from Derraid, Tombain, Clashendeugle and Kichanroy to Uchtogorm and Craigdhu.

Caochan Cumhann: The narrow, strait stream NJ 0376 3260
Caochan Camhann

A burn rising north of Uchtugorm and flowing in a south westerly direction until it joins Allt an Fhithich at Lower Derraid. [OSNB]

Caochannaneun: Stream of the birds NJ 0715 3192 Cuchaneun 1851, Cuchanuane 1901

A small one storey dwelling house, thatched and in fair condition. [OSNB]

Caochan nan Eun: Stream of the birds NJ 0731 3217

A small stream rising a little north of Caochannaneun, flowing south westerly and joining Allt Breac. [OSNB]

Caochan Ruadh: Red stream NJ 0477 3360

A small burn west of Easter Kichanroy and flowing in a south easterly direction until it joins the Allt Breac. [OSNB]

Carn a' Ghille Chearr: Hill of the left handed lad NJ 0415 3568
Carn auch Gillie Cheir, 1810

A rugged hill situated a little south west of Huntly's Cave. [OSNB]

Carn an Loin: Hill of the marsh NJ 0701 3610

A hill covered with heathy pasture, situated about one mile to the north west of Cairn an Fhradhairc. [OSNB]

Carn na Croiche: Hill of the gallows   NJ 0223 3313

A large wooded hill lying on the east side of the old Highland Railway line, five miles north of Grantown. Tradition says that this was an ancient place of execution. Human remains were found here in 1865. [OSNB] Last known execution was in 1704 and recorded that gallows were repaired in 1735.

Carn na Croiche Plantation: NJ 0221 3336

Castle Grant: NJ 0413 3018   Bail a'chaisteil   [OSNB]

The old name for Castle Grant was Bail a'chaisteil, used in charters until 1694, when the area became the Regality of Grant. It then became known as Castle Grant after the clan.

Fields around Castle Grant: Croftis of Ballachastell, Makrobbie's Croft 1611, Makgeorge Croft 1611, Makgowin's Croft 1611. Collochcastle 1750, Cuil a Chastal   1809, Gardener's House 1750, Cretoch Robert 1750, Croft McRobert, Ochku More, Luragan, Black Waird, The Clover Park, Well Park, Old Garden, Little Park, Dallas Park, Millar's Croft, Garden Croft , Horse Park, Garkeen Park. 1809

Castle Grant Laundry: NJ 0428 3010   Washing House 1770

Castle Grant, Seafield Memorial Stone: NJ 0461 3050

Situated within a fenced copse of pine trees in the Deer Park.

Clash an Dunain: Hollow or ravine of the small hill or fort   NJ 0528 3171   Den of Clashendunan 1767, Clais an Dunan 1812

A small picturesque, wooded glen extending south west of Balnaclash. [OSNB] Named after the fort which overlooks the ravine.

Clais Gharbh: Rough ravine or hollow NJ 0791 3257

A hollow between Knockannakeist and Culfoichmore.

Clais Mhor: Large hollow NJ 0692 3321

A hollow on the face of Tom Mor. [OSNB]

Clasbeg: 1771 Little hollow NJ 058 290

Clashendeugle: Hollow of the rye NJ 0342 3351 Clashendugle 1767, Clashendugle 1802, Glash Shogle 1810, Clashdokle 1841, Clashinteukle 1851

A farmhouse and out offices each of which are one storey high thatched and in good repair. [OSNB]

Field: Clashendugle 1802

Easter Cottartown: Settlement of the cottars NJ 0351 3117

A farmhouse and out offices one storey high, thatched and in good repair. [OSNB]

Wester Cottartown: NJ 0353 3099

A farmhouse and out offices one storey high, thatched and in good repair. [OSNB]

Cottartown Belts: NJ 0335 3083

Craggan Brechk: 1810 Stony brae NJ 0457 3542

Cragganmore Wood: NJ 0438 3227

Craggens: 1809 NJ 041 287

Creagan Mor: Large rocky place NJ 0424 3249 Tom Bain 1802, Craig More 1810, Craggan Mor

A prominent hill now covered in trees about one mile north of Castle Grant. [OSNB]

Craigbeg: Little rock NJ 0369 3236 Craig Beg 1810

A farmhouse and out offices, one storey high, thatched and in good repair. [OSNB]

Fields: Lack Cuchan, Lack a Vall Creiachan 1810

Croft of Craigbegg: 1767   NJ 0357 3243

Fields: Miklefield, Hens Bush 1802

Craigdhu: Black rock   NJ 0385 3203   Craig Du 1810

A croft house with suitable out offices, one storey high, thatched and in good repair. [OSNB]

Field: Creiach More 1810

Creag an Fhitich: Raven's craig   NJ 0233 3271   Craig Neich 1807

A high precipitous rock over hanging Allt an Fhithich, directly south of Carn na Croiche. [OSNB]

Cree Dearg: Red boundary   NJ 0385 3485   Hee Darg 1767

A craggy hill lying south west of Carn a' Ghille Chearr and south east of Carn Bad na Caorach. [OSNB]

Culfoichmore: 1767   Large cup shaped hollow   NJ 0878 3226

A farm steading and dwelling house, one storey high thatched and in good repair. [OSNB]

Wester Culfoich: Cup shaped hollow   NJ 0828 3200

A farm steading and dwelling house, one storey high, thatched and in middling repair. [OSNB]

Deer Park: NJ 0442 3031

Once an extensive grass park situated close to Castle Grant in which a herd of deer were kept. It is landscaped with isolated trees and woodland.

Delliefure: Haugh of the pasture land

Cuarst of Dellifure: Round hollow of Dellifure   NJ 0840 3067 1851, Courst 1861

A cottage one storey high, thatched and in middling repair. [OSNB]

Delliefure Burn: NJ 0829 3154

Delliefure Clumps: NJ 0692 3089

Delliefure Cottage: NJ 0721 30390

A one storey cottage with suitable office houses, thatched and in middling condition.

[OSNB]

Lower Dellifour: 1851   NJ 0763 3069   Wester Delliefure

Middle Dellifour: 1851   NJ 0701 3107

Easter Delliefure: 1851   NJ 0777 3135   Easter Dellifour 1810

A farm steading and dwelling house, one storey high, thatched and middling repair, partly in ruin. [OSNB]

Fields: The Sparden, The Dale, Dalln Fat 1810

Wester Delliefure: NJ 0763 3069   Lower Delliefure 1851, 1901

A farm steading and dwelling house, one storey high, slated and in good repair. [OSNB]

Fields: Khean Eris-a-Uall, Crait Brunach 1810

Mains of Delliefure: NJ 0676 3146   Daillefoure 1611, Upper Dillifure 1767, Upper Dellifour 1851, 1901

A farmhouse, steading and offices, two storeys high, slated and in fair condition. [OSNB]

Fields: Crait na Cardich, The Loch, Ballnellan, Wester Field, Rue na Chuit, Mela Fleuch, Dreim e Cruy, Dreim More 1810

Milton of Delliefure: NJ 0766 3094   Milton of Dellifour 1851

A farm steading and dwelling house one storey high thatched and in good repair. [OSNB]

School of Dellifure: 1851   NJ 0632 3198

Delriach: The greyish or brindled field   NJ 0559 3451

A farm steading and dwelling house, one storey high, thatched and in middling repair. [OSNB]

Lower Derraid: The long grove   NJ 0352 3255   Burnside Cottage 1891, Smithy Croft 1891

A croft house and out offices, one storey high, thatched and in good repair. [OSNB]

Middle Derraid: 1810

Fields: Knockan Yeorn 1810

Upper Derraid: NJ 0278 3310   Park of Dirryrait 1767 Bard-n'daoire-raid 1838

Applied to two farm steadings and dwelling houses, all of which are one storey high, thatched and in good repair. [OSNB]

Fields: Bruick Ual, Bog Fearn, Crait a Chlay 1810

Dreim Dunan: 1809   Ridge of the little hill or fort   NJ 0521 3103 The Black Park of Drumdunan 1750

A ruined croft.

Drumindunan Wood: NJ 0513 3043

Dunan: The little hill or fort   NJ 0541 3119,   NJ 0548 3136 Downan 1611

Two ruined crofts

Freuchy: Descriptive name; place of heather, for the lands belonging to the Laird of Grant around Castle Grant.

Freuchie's Hillock: Heathery hillock   NJ 0452 3012   Fruchie Hillock Parks 1750, Freuchie Hillock 1750, Cnoc an Fruich, Freuchy Hillock 1809.

A small circular mound situated within the Deer Park at Castle Grant. [OSNB] A Class 1 Pictish stone, now in the National Museum of Scotland was found here.

Garbh-ath Mor: The large rough ford   NJ 0763 2925

A ford on the River Spey, situated northwest of the farmstead of Starindeye. Tradition points to this as being the spot where the government army forded the River Spey on their march to the battle at the Haughs of Cromdale in 1690. [OSNB]

Gardener's House: NJ 0470 2933

Gamekeepers Wood: NJ 0423 3141

Garrow's Bridge: NJ 0520 2924

Named after the Garrow family who were millers at the neighbouring Milton of Castle Grant.

Garthkeen: Head of the enclosure   NJ 0417 3131   Garthkeen Park 1801, Gartkeen 1809.

Field: The Clover Park 1812

A croft house with suitable out offices one storey high thatched, in good repair. [OSNB]

Long been the residence of the head gamekeeper for Castle Grant.

Glaschoile: NJ 0283 3224   The grey green wood   Glasschile Improvements 1801, Glasschile 1802, Glaschoil 1871, Moss of Glaschyle 1801 [OSNB]

Grant's Fort: NJ 0534 3159

A little motte overlooking Clash Dunan. Tradition says it was an early Grant fortification.

Grant Town: NJ 0376 2949   Bail na Granndach, Grantown Roy, Old Grantown 1809, Old Grantown Park 1809, Lands of Old Grantown 1812

Original settlement close to Castle Grant. Replaced by the current town in 1765, and reports state old village was finally abandoned by 1823.

Old Grantown Wood: NJ 0365 2935

Head of Scor Guie: 1812   NJ 060 366

Rising ground east of the rock of the wind

Heathfield: NJ 0392 2843

This name is applied to a dwelling house and farm steading, two storeys high, slated and in good repair. [OSNB]

Former home of James Grant, clerk to Sir James Grant.

Home Farm: NJ 0394 3054   Barns of Castle Grant 1851

Applied to the farm steading situated about 14 chains north of Castle Grant, it is from one to two storeys high, slated and in good repair. [OSNB]

Huntly's Cave: NJ 0469 3598

A small hole on the summit of the rock overlooking the ravine of Allt an Fhithich. Named after George 2nd Marquis of Huntly, who supported the cause of Charles 1. It is said the 3rd Marquis likewise hid here, kept alive by the Laird of Grant's sister who he later married. [OSNB]

Huntly's Cave: NJ 0469 3598

Situated in the Uaigh Mhor. It's a small space, completely covered over by a large stone. It's said that one of the lords of Huntly found refuge here while proscribed by the government. [OSNB]

Huntly's Cave Cottages: NJ 0180 3319   Sassenach's Hut   1871

Former houses for railway surface men and their families on the Highland Railway. Now demolished.

Easter Kichanroy: Red stream   NJ 0406 3402 Cuchan Ruag 1810

A farmhouse and out offices each of which are one storey high, thatched and in good repair. [OSNB]

Wester Kichanroy: Red stream   NJ 0390 3380   Cuchan Ruag 1810

A farmhouse and out offices each of which are one storey high, thatched and in good repair. [OSNB]

Knockannacardich: Little hillock of the smith   NJ 0685 3284 Knockanakeardich 1767, Town of Knocknacardich 1802, Knock na Cardich 1810

A small farmhouse and steading, one storey high, thatched and in good condition. [OSNB]

Fields: Black Drum, Wet Leys, Hard Leys, Black Hillock. 1802

Fields: Toum More, The Drum, Blaar More, Lackan Uaran, Bual McHomash, Rue n Leish. 1810

Knockannakeist: Little hillock of the chest or coffin   NJ 0749 3258 Knockankeist 1611, Knockanakiest 1767

A farm steading and dwelling house, one storey high, thatched and in middling repair. [OSNB] A stone coffin or cist was believed to have been found here.

Fields: Long windings, improvement called Burd Strype 1802

Knockanruich: 1809   Little heathery hillock   NJ 0462 2900   Knockanrich 1771,   Cnockanruich 1804, Knockenruich, Knockanruich 1812.

Knock Urich: NJ 047 308   Mole hillock

Lag na Dothich: NJ 0703 3016

A large inverted conical depression in the wood. Possibly a kettle hole from glacial activity, the feature was used to pen cattle at night. It's situated beside Tom a' Bheathaich, hillock of the byre.   [OSNB]

Lagg: (Achnarrowbeag)   The hollow   NJ 0385 3282

A farmhouse and out offices, one storey high, partly thatched, in good repair. [OSNB]

Lodge (East): NJ 0329 3020   Green Gate 1809, Porter's Lodge 1871

Baronial style lodge and railway halt. Built in 1863 by the Inverness & Perth Junction Railway Company in thanks to 7th Earl of Seafield, for allowing them to run the railway line through his estate. [OSNB]

Lodge (West):   NJ 0352 2883   Porter Lodge 1851, Porter's Lodge 1871, South Porter's Lodge

A cottage at south entrance to Castle Grant, two storeys high, slated and in good repair. [OSNB]

Entrance to drive for Castle Grant from the Grantown side.

Lyngarrie: 1851   Rough meadow or enclosure   NJ 0592 3383 Lyngarrie 1861

A dwelling house one storey high, thatched and in good repair. [OSNB]

Lynmore: The large meadow or enclosure   NJ 0369 3165

A farmhouse and out offices one storey high, the former slated, the latter thatched, all in good repair. [OSNB]

Field: Torrin Buie 1810

Lynmore Cottage: NJ 0381 3173

Lower Lynmore Wood: NJ 0356 3192

Mid Lynmore Wood: NJ 0340 3154

Upper Lynemore Wood: NJ 0291 3186

Lyntaurie: Summer meadow or enclosure   NJ 0554 3528
Improvements of Meikle and Little Lensouries 1767, Lyn Taurie 1810

A dwelling house, one storey high and in miserable condition. [OSNB]

Maitan: The meadow   Miadan, Meudan

Name of a croft near the Port.

Mein improvement:

Near Upper Delliefure.

Mill of Castle Grant: (corn)   NJ 0518 2928   The Milne & Milntoune of Ballachastell 1611

A corn mill, farmhouse and out offices, one storey high, thatched, in good repair. [OSNB]

Milton Wood: NJ 0441 2973

Port: A Ferry

East Port: NJ 0712 2939   Eister Port 1611

A farm house and out offices from one to two storeys high, partly thatched and partly slated in good repair. [OSNB]

Field: The Back, The Barn Field, Haugh Ground 1771

Mid Port: NJ 0650 2958   Mid Port 1611

A farm house and out offices one storey high, thatched and in good repair. [OSNB]

Nether Port: NJ 0609 2863   Lower Port 1851, 1901,

A farmhouse and out offices, one storey high, thatched and in good repair. [OSNB]

Upper Port: NJ 0556 2907

A farmhouse and out offices one storey high thatched in good repair. [OSNB]

Upper Port Standing Stones: NJ 0540 2914

An alignment of two standing stones, NW to SE and a second pair stand close together, adjacent to the farm. [OSNB]

Upper Port Wood: NJ 0590 2925

West Port: NJ 0645 2810   Wester Port 1611, Wester Port 1901

A farm steading consisting of dwelling house and office houses all one storey high and in good condition. [OSNB]

Fields: Haugh of West Port 1771

Poul a Chor: The pool of the hollow   NJ 0347 2960   1812, Moss of Polochur, 1802

Drained about 1802

Pulchor Belts: NJ 0331 2931

Raitt: NJ 0556 2948

A croft house one storey high, thatched in good repair. [OSNB]

Roman Road: see Via Regia [OSNB]

Rue Vourslich: 1810   NJ 0500 3576

A moss near Lyntourie, below the road passing Huntly's Cave.

Sassenachs Hut: See Huntly's Cave Cottages   NJ 0180 3319

Sgor Gaoithe: Windy Rock   NJ 0523 3617   Sgor Gaothach, Scur Guie, 1810

A prominent peak situated on the watershed a short distance eastward of Huntly's Cave. Good views to the south over Strathspey towards the Cairngorms and north over the Dava Moor towards the Black Isle and beyond. [OSNB]

Sheanmore Improvements: 1780   Large fairy hill   NJ 0627 3109

Sir James's Well: 1770   NJ 0477 3045

A ruined well structure beside the Deer Park, associated with Sir James Grant.

Slochd: Deep hollow   NJ 0257 3267   Mukle Calms 1802

The grassy meadow beneath Huntly's Cave, enclosed on all sides by rock and steep banks.

Stron na Grandich: Grant's nose or promontory   NJ 0259 3270

The Banks: 1771   NJ 062 291

Steep braes between Upper Port and Boat of Cromdale on north side of road.

Tobar na Danich: The Sunday well   NJ 0542 2901

Visited by folk from further up the parish on way to Cromdale Church.

Tobar Ma'Luaig: St Luac's Well   NJ 0658 2899

A spring situated on the northern bank of the River Spey, nearly opposite to the Church of Cromdale. It is now just a sandy patch on the embankment. [OSNB]

Tom a' Bheathaich: Hillock of the byre   NJ 0724 3023   Tomvaich 1771

The byre is a large inverted conical depression in the wood. Possibly a kettle hole from glacial activity, the feature was used to pen cattle at night. [OSNB]

Tombain: 1771   White hillock   NJ 0650 2929

Tombain: White Hill   NJ 0320 3345   Tombain 1767, Toum Baan 1810

Applied to two farm steadings and dwelling houses, all of which are one storey high, partly slated and partly thatched and in good repair. [OSNB]

Fields: Mickle face, Gortens 1802

Fields: Tor Vounie, Tor Veallie, Buall Du 1810

Tombain Plantation: NJ 0394 3441

Tombuie: 1771   Yellow hillock   NJ 065 292

Tom Mor: Large hillock   NJ 0719 3382

Situated ¾ of a mile east of Knock of Auchnahannet, with a transmitter pylon on the summit.

Tomnabae: 1802   Hillock of the birch tree   NJ 064 289

Tomvaich: Hillock of the byre   NJ 0657 3042   1771, 1851

A farm steading consisting of two dwelling houses and three office houses, all one storey high and in middling condition. [OSNB]

Lower Tomvaich Wood: NJ 0676 3018   Plantation called Tomvaich 1771

Upper Tomvaich Wood: NJ 0608 3036

Moss of Tomvaich: 1771   NJ 071 299

Torran Ban: 1802   The white hillock   NJ 0693 3285

Conical glacial knoll, site of a Bronze or Iron Age fort. [OSNB]

Torran a Chat: 1810   Little hillock of the cat   NJ 0514 3417

Torron na Grunich: 1810   NJ 048 428

Situated in wood behind Auchnarrowmore school house.

Uaigh Mhor: Large grave   NJ 0471 3597

A hollow shaped like a dug grave, on the ridge between Sgor Ghaothaich and Carn ' Ghille Chearr. [OSNB]

Uchtubeg: Little hillside   NJ 0468 3175   Auchtobegg 1767, Ochku Beg 1810, Ouchtobeg 1861

A farmhouse and out offices partly thatched and partly slated and from one to two storeys high, in good repair. [OSNB]

Fields: Ochku Beg, Touper Fy, Tau Toumack, Uiten a Bruich 1810

Uchtugorm: Blue, green hillside   NJ 0394 3284   Auchtogorm 1767, Ochku Gorum 1810, Uchtogorum 1901

A farmhouse and out offices one storey high, thatched and in good repair. [OSNB]

Field: Barn Fold 1802

Fields: Bual Du, Brae Vatt, Peaul na Ha, Loin Press Keaunich 1810

Via Regia: King's Highway   NJ 0480 3472

A very old road once crossed the River Spey at Garbha Mhor and followed the current road to above Auchnagallin. It continues beyond there by Huntly's Cave and onto the Ourack. It was possibly a Via Regia or King's Road dating as far back as the 12th century, which linked Strathspey to Forres and Elgin in the medieval period. On some maps it is recorded as Roman, but there is no evidence for this and was the view of 19th century antiquarians.

Huntly's Cave

Walks

From the West Lodge of Castle Grant walk along the drive to Castle Grant continuing in the same direction, as the main drive veers right. Follow the track to a stone dyke and field. Here can be seen all that's left of Old Grantown, former settlement for Castle Grant and falling into decline when new Grantown was established in 1765. The following year the remaining inhabitants marched with sprigs of pine, the Grant clan badge and oxen hauled the mercat cross to the new town, where about the hospital brae, they were greeted by the new inhabitants. Little survives of the former settlement other than a few scattered stones and the mercat cross has long since mysteriously disappeared.

Returning to the drive or head across the field to the right, where a gate gives access to the drive. A little further Castle Grant appears through the trees. Home to the chiefs of clan Grant since the 16th century, the castle has had a chequered history in recent decades. Continue through the avenue of trees until on the right appears the former Home Farm for the Castle. Veer to the right past the farm and turn to look right at the famous Adam brothers' addition to Castle Grant. This stark, plain granite face did not impress Queen Victoria on her visit in 1860, writing in her diary that it resembled a factory.

The track heads north and through some imposing gate pillars where you might be welcomed by the noise from the gamekeepers kennels. Garthkeen has long been the head keeper's residence for the Castle Grant part of Seafield estate. Follow on with birch trees on the right and fields on the left, past the small wooden cottage of Lynmore, where the track ends at a gate and the main road. Go left passed Lynmore and a sign for the Dava Way appears. Joining the route here leads through the atmospheric Mid Lynmore Wood to re-join the railway line at Glaschoil. A little further a sign and information board directs the path down to Huntly's Cave, a site now often frequented by budding rock climbers. The return route can be by the Dava Way to the bridge above the West Lodge or to a track that leads from the main road to Castle Grant just before Ballieward. This returns by the castle to the West Lodge.

For a route less travelled that visits sites steeped with Clan Grant connections, start at the West Lodge and walk to the bridge just before the entrance to Castle Grant. Turn right and walk straight ahead. From this path when the trees have fewer leaves, a good view of Castle Grant is revealed. A little further on is the old laundry house and a gate beside the wood. Cross the gate and follow the fence by the wood and on the left a green mound appears just at the corner of the wood. This is Freuchie Hillock, a site where a Class 1 Pictish Stone was discovered. It is a beautiful, simple carving of a stag and is now on display in the National Museum of Scotland. The hillock overlooks the former deer park and a wooded copse in the distance has memorials erected to the memory of members of the Seafield Family.

Follow the fence and track skirting the wood to the right will lead to the main track through the wood. Cross bridges over the Allt a'Bhacain and Allt an Fhithich. Take a left turn and head north through the thickly wooded area. This follows the Allt an Fhithich upstream, though it is mostly hidden by the trees. The path comes to a cross roads, take the track to the right slightly up hill to a field and large stone dike. Cross the field to an avenue of mature trees and down to the left appears Clash an Dunan. This natural feature is a steeply wooded ravine, secluded and holding a strong defensive position. On the lip of the ravine a small hillock is all that remains of Grant's Fort. Though associated with the clan, it could be much older and been constructed by a previous occupier of these lands. A little beyond the fort, a farm track descends into the clash and up the other side, beneath the fields of Balnaclash to join the main road to Auchnagallin.

Turn left and walk a little way past the entrance to Balnaclash and turn left to Auchnarrowmore. This farm has very old connections to the clan Ciaran branch of Clan Grant and was once part of a larger davoch of the same name. Follow the road round past the old Auchnarrow school house and on the right beside the plantation is a gate. Through the gate a firebreak leads to eventually open at the corner of a field with views towards Uchtugorm, the Braes of Castle Grant and Huntly's Cave. The forest trail ends at the road to The Braes a little east of Uchtugorm. Turn left and follow the road west to a junction with a road sign listing the names of the farms in the vicinity. A steep road to the right leads up hill to Derraid, Tombain and Clashendeugle, but it's worth it for the views south towards the Cairngorms and Cromdale Hills. The Braes were once a close knit community with their own mill and blacksmith. Cummings, Calders, Mackenzies and Grants were the principle families. To return walk by the road to Lynmore and follow the options in walk one from there.

3: Allt Breac Circuit

This walk is mostly on road and level tracks. Begin at the head of the valley above Wester Achnagallin. There is a parking space on the right beside a gate. The track through the gate heading north is an ancient route to and from Strathspey and believed to be a Via Regia or King's Road, possibly dating back to the 12th century. As the road swings to the right towards the top, a rowan tree in a gully is a good spot to leave the track and look for the less well known Huntly's Cave. The gully is well named the Uaigh Mor or large grave for it is shaped like one. Among the gorse bushes on the left are some large boulders forming a small cave to shelter a fugitive. Not a deep large cave in the traditional sense. Return to the track and head on a bit further, eventually arriving at another gate. This is the watershed; Strathspey to your back, and The Dava, Ourack and as far as the Moray Firth, Black Isle and hills in Sutherland to the north. The rocky outcrop to the right is Sgor Gaoithe, the point or rock of the wind. A great spot to sit and take in the view.

Return to the main road where parked and follow the road clockwise past Easter and Wester Auchnagallin and over the Allt Breac. Next pass the turn off to Knock of Auchnahannet and Auchnahannet. This Gaelic name is quite common and signifies there was once an early church or chapel in the vicinity. Old maps place a field name called the chapel to the left of the road near Ballinlagg. A little further on a track to the left leads up to the forest edge and a large green mound that is visible from miles away. This is Torran Ban or the white hillock and is the remains of an Iron Age fort. Beside it are the ruins of Knockanacardich, the hillock of the smith. Well worth a closer look. The forest trail continues to skirt the wood south to Knockannakeist, hillock of the chest or coffin, again substantial ruins remain. Return to the main road and follow it round past Upper Delliefure and at the T junction turn right to return past Wester Achnagallin. If desired it's possible to turn left before Balnaclash to join walk two.

The Cairngorms from The Via Regia or King's Highway

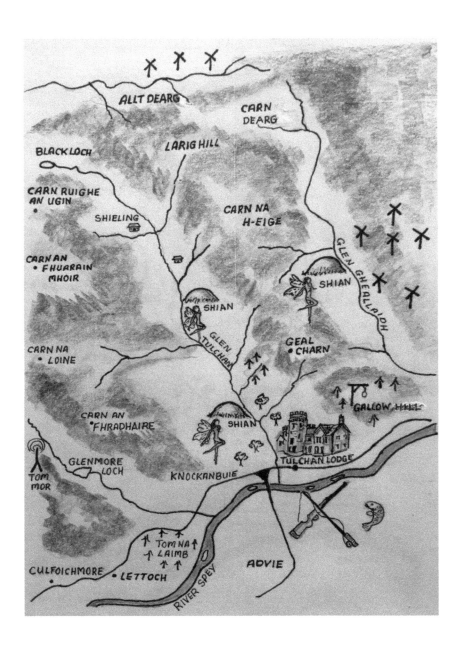

CHAPTER 5

Tulchan

Davochs 1773

Davoch of Tulchen

Calendar, Polcreach, Balwaddan, Delcroy, Stra'an, Knocktulchen, Knockanbuie, Culdryan, Culdorachmore, Culdorachbegg, Altyoullie improvements, Rynanuan improvement, Lynvaich improvement, Dorriemore improvements, Corriebuie improvement, Kichannahiollar improvement, Culghruanan improvement.

Davoch of Culquoichmore

Wester Lettoch, Easter Lettoch, Laglia, Culquoichmore, Doirrie improvement.

Allt a' Choire Bhuidhe: Yellow hollow burn   NJ 0891 3829

A burn rising in a small hollow from which it takes its name. It is about a quarter of a mile in length and flows westward into Dubh-allt Mor. [OSNB]

Allt a' Chuiach: Burn of the quaich or hollow   NJ 1046 3377

Appears only on modern Ordnance Survey maps. It is the same burn as the Allt na Luachair, which on older Ordnance Survey and estate maps is called this for its full length from source to the Spey. It forms part of the boundary of the Cairngorms National Park.

Allt a' Gheallaidh: Burn of brightness, glistening, clear   NJ 1291 3849   Ault Gauie 1804

This burn drains Glen Gheallaidh. Formed by the junction of Caochan Aonach and Allt Clais a Gobhar, it flows southward for about two miles and then eastward for another four and after a course of six miles enters the River Spey. Its principal tributaries are Allt Bealaidh, Caochan na Sul Dubh, Allt Mhonadh, Allt Cas and Allt Loch Mhadudh. It is commonly written, Burn of Aldyoulie and by some, thought to mean the Devil's Burn. Others say burn of covenant or promise. [OSNB]

Allt a' Mhadaidh: Burn of the dog   NJ 1374 3738   Caochan Ault Vattie 1804, Allt Loch Mhadadh

A small burn rising a little north of Carn na Croiche and after a north easterly course of about three quarters of a mile becomes confluent with Allt a'Gheallaidh, which formed the boundary between Knockando and Cromdale parishes. [OSNB]

Allt an Loin Mhor: Burn of the large marsh, bog   NJ 0879 3637 Loin More 1804

A long burn rising on the eastern side of Carn an Fhuarain Mhoir in the former County of Inverness and flowing eastward into Moray, discharging its waters into the Burn of Tulchan. It formed the county boundary between the counties of Inverness and Moray from its source for half its course. [OSNB]

Allt Bad an Eich: Burn of the clump of the horse   NJ 0928 3462

A small burn arising from three small streams, a short distance to the west of Creag a'Bharain and running southerly until it joins Allt na Luachair. [OSNB]

Allt Clachach: Burn of the stone or stony stream   NJ 1146 3871 Cuchan na Clachmore 1804

A small mountain burn rising on the north side of Geal Charn and flowing in a northerly direction for about three quarters of a mile, where it flows into Allt Gheallaidh. [OSNB]

Allt Clachach Beag: Little stony stream   NJ 1170 3849   Cuchan na Clach Beg 1804

A small burn of about a quarter of a mile in length and flowing into Allt Clachach. [OSNB]

Allt Clais na Gaibhre: Burn of the goat hollow   NJ 1050 4147

A small burn flowing from a lochan in Clais Gobhar and taking a southward course for about half a mile joins Caochan Aonaich. The joint waters of these two burns form the start of Allt Gheallaidh. [OSNB]

Allt Dearg: Red Burn   NJ 0783 4118   Burn of Ault Dearg 1775, Ault Dearg 1812

A burn which rises on the north side of Carn Dearg and runs westwards for about two miles where it flows into the Ourack Burn. During the greater part of its course it formed part of the boundary between the former counties of Inverness-shire and Moray. [OSNB]

Allt Dubh: The black burn   NJ 0822 4119   Cichan du-na-Lairg

1775, Cuchan Du 1804

A small stream rising at the north western base of Larig Hill and flowing in a north westerly direction until it joins Allt Dearg about ¾ mile from its source. [OSNB]

Allt Loch Mhadaidh:	Burn of the wolf or dog loch NJ 1366 3735

A small stream flowing from Loch Mhadadh, from which it derives its name and flowing eastward eventually into Allt Gheallaidh. [OSNB]

Allt Lonn Beag:	Little burn of the marsh or bog NJ 0821 3788	Loin Veck 1804

A burn rising on the east side of Carn Ruigh an Uain and flowing eastward into the Burn of Tulchan. Its principal tributary is Allt Ruigh an Uain. [OSNB]

Allt na Bealaidh:	Burn of the broom NJ 0991 4055	Cuchan Byallie 1804

A burn rising on the south side of Carn Dearg and flowing a mile eastwards into Allt Gheallaidh. [OSNB]

Allt na Luachair:	Burn of the rushes NJ 0784 3419

A considerable sized burn, rising in a flat marshy bog lying about half a mile to the west of Carn a Loin and running generally easterly for about six miles, where it joins the River Spey. The boundary of the Cairngorms National Park follows it until joins Allt a' Chuiach. [OSNB]

Allt Ruighe an Uain:	Burn of the lamb shieling NJ 0819 3819	Cuchan Rynan Uan 1804

A burn flowing from the east side of the hill from which it derives its name. The burn takes an easterly course and after a run of about a mile flows in Allt Lonn Beag. [OSNB]

An Sithean:	Fairy hillock NJ 1076 3642

A small hillock behind the farm of Culdorachmore, on the hill road up Glen Tulchan. [OSNB]

Bad an Eich:	Horse's tuft or place frequented by horses NJ 0871 3576	Carnaheileck 1770, Cairn na Hellick 1810

A small round topped hill over which the former county boundary crossed. It is covered with heathy pasture and lies a short distance to the north of the stream of the same name. [OSNB]

Badinlochan: Little clumps of the lochan. Possibly in the area of NJ 095 420

Recorded on Pont's map with a note that a fight took place here between clan Grant and clan Chattan (McIntosh). Must have been prior to 1590's.

Ballan na Gaun: 1804   Little farmstead of the smith   NJ 1067 3645

Balnacraobh: Farmstead of the tree   NJ 1422 3635   Balnacruie 1804, Balnacreigh 1851, Balnacrey 1861

A small farm steading situated a little south of Polcreach. [OSNB]

Balnruich: 1804   Farmstead of the heather   NJ 0963 3701

Balvattan: Farmstead of the little clumps   NJ 1412 3621 Ballwaddan 1804, Balvattan 1901

A crofter's dwelling house of one storey in good repair. [OSNB]

Battearick: 1804   Clump of pasture   NJ 1384 3771

Two ruined farm houses with enclosure.

Blaar Dir Lea: 1810   Moss of the grey grove   NJ 093 331

Blaar na Larig: 1812   Moss of the pass   NJ 0801 4031

Black Loch: NJ 0646 3909   Loch Cuchan Lochan 1812

A small picturesque loch, between Carn Ruigh an Uain and Carn Gharbh-aite, from which flows the Black Loch Burn. [OSNB]

Black Loch Burn: NJ 0726 3896

A burn flowing from the Black Loch in a south easterly course for about a mile, where it joins Dubh-allt Mor. The joint burns then take the name Burn of Tulchan. [OSNB]

Black Stripe: Black stream or ditch   NJ 1031 4133   Caochan Du 1808

A stream of about half a mile in length. It is the first tributary of Allt Gheallaidh. Stripe is a Scots word for a ditch or small stream. [OSNB]

Burn of Tulchan: NJ 1162 3644   Burn of Tulchen 1804

A large burn from the waters of the various streams that drain Glen Tulchan. It is formed by the junction of Dubh Allt Mor with Black

Loch Burn and its principal tributaries are: Allt Lonn Mor, Allt Lon Beag and various smaller streams. It flows into the Spey after a course of about five miles. [OSNB]

Black Loch

Callender: 1851   NJ 1474 3687

A good substantial farm steading and dwelling house of one storey in good repair. [OSNB]

Field: Craitn-lone. 1804

Craig of Callender: 1804   NJ 1456 3696

A prominent hill covered with large boulders and stones a little north of the farm of Callender. [OSNB]

Woods of Callender: NJ 1489 3663

A narrow belt of wood situated on the north bank of the Spey, a little north of the farms of Polcreach and Callender. [OSNB]

Caochan Aonaich: Burn of the hill or height   NJ 1020 4174 Cichan Neannich 1775

A burn of about a mile in length, which rises at the head of Glen Gheallaidh and flowing south east, joins with Allt a Gheallaidh. [OSNB]

Caochan Daraich: Burn of the oak tree NJ 1115 3700 Caochan Darach 1804

A burn rising on the south side of Geal Charn and after a run southward of about three quarters of a mile flows into the Burn of Tulchan. [OSNB]

Caochan du na Larig: 1812 Burn of the pass

Caochan Loisgte: Burnt stream NJ 0895 3421

A small hill stream which rises at the south western base of Carn an Fhradhairc and flowing south east until it empties into Allt na Luachair. It is about a mile and a half long. [OSNB]

Caochan Luachrach: The burn of rushes NJ 0703 4081 Cichan Glenbrachk 1775

A small burn rising at the south western base of Larig Hill and flowing in a westerly direction, until it joins Allt Dearg, about ¾ of a mile from the junction of Allt Dubh. [OSNB]

Caochan na h-Iolaire: Burn of the eagle NJ 0960 3765 Cuchan na Heulre 1804

A burn rising on the southwest side of Carn Eag, flowing in a south westerly direction and into the Burn of Tulchan after a run of about ¼ of a mile. [OSNB]

Caochan na h-Iolaire Shieling: NJ 0954 3757

Caochan na Sula Duibhe: Stream of the black eye NJ 0911 3665

A small stream of about 1/4 a mile in length, flowing into Allt Lonn Mor and dividing Geal Charn from Creig Phigeidh. [OSNB]

Caochan na Sula Duibhe: Stream of the black eye NJ 1131 3942 Cuchan Sulduie 1804

A burn flowing from the east side of the Larig Hill and into Allt Gheallaidh, after a course of nearly half a mile. [OSNB]

Caochan Ruadh: Red stream NJ 1091 3581

A small burn rising a little south of the hill Cul Dorcha, and after a south easterly course of about a mile and a quarter, flows into the River Spey. [OSNB]

Caochan Sron na Saobhaidhe: Stream of the fox's nose or promontory NJ 1054 3716

A burn rising between Carn Eag and Geal Charn and flowing southward for ¾ of a mile where it joins the Burn of Tulchan. [OSNB]

Carn a Luchar: 1810   Hill of the rushes   NJ 0792 3502   (see Carn an Fhradhairc).

Carn a Suvie: 1804   Fox hill   NJ 1091 3819

Carn an Fhradhairc: Hill of the good view   NJ 0792 3502   Carn-a-Luachar 1810 (Hill of Rushes)

A large and prominent hill covered with heath and rather rocky on its southern side.   [OSNB] Its name has changed on modern Ordnance Survey maps. Previously Carn-a-Luachar, from which a burn of the same name flows.

Carn an Fhuarain Mhoir: Large spring hill   NJ 0664 3692 [OSNB]

Appears as Gyall Carn (1812) on earlier maps, which is now given to an adjacent top.

Carn Bathearick: 1804   Hill of the pasture clump   NJ 1220 3805

Not named on modern Ordnance Survey maps.

Carn Cuchan na Cruve: 1812   Hill of the tree burn

Carn Dearg: Red Hill   NJ 0922 4128

This name is given to a piece of high ground at the head of Allt Dearg and on the western boundary of the former county of Moray. [OSNB]

Carn Domhnaich: Sunday hill   NJ 1036 3603

A hill in the parish of Advie and west of the farm of Knocktulchan. [OSNB]

Carn Du Ault: 1812   Black burn hill   NJ 0958 3963   Carn Duault 1804,

Carn Feurach nan Each: Hill of the horses pasture   NJ 0965 3584

Hill ground, covered with heather on the south side of Allt Lonn Mor and opposite Creig Phigeidh. [OSNB]

Carn Gharbh-Aite: Hill of the rough place   NJ 0625 3877   Hill of Gervill, Knock Garabit 1812, Carn Gharbh-baid

A prominent hill situated at the head of Glen Tulchen and over the top of which passed the boundary between Moray and Inverness-shire. [OSNB]

Carn Lochan: 1812   Hill of the small loch   NJ 0723 3986

Carn na Croiche: Gallow Hill   NJ 1307 3691   Toum na Croich 1804

An extensive hill overlooking the Dale of Advie and Glen Gheallaidh and according to tradition was the place where criminals were executed. [OSNB] Now known as Gallow Hill on modern Ordnance Survey maps.

Carn na Culechdu: 1804   NJ 1010 3736

Carn na Doire: Hill of the grove   NJ 0918 3350   Carn Dir 1810

A small hill about half a mile south of Allt na Luachair. [OSNB]

Carn na h-Eige: Hill of the nick or gap   NJ 0984 3870   Carn Rerick 1804, Carna Heick 1804

A high hill on the south east side of the Larig Hill and east of Burn of Tulchan. [OSNB]

Carn Ruighe an Uain: Hill of the lamb shieling   NJ 0657 3794 Carn Rin Uan 1804, Carn Rein Uan 1812

A prominent hill on the north western side of Advie parish and over the top of which passed the boundary between counties of Moray and Inverness-shire. [OSNB]

Carn Sheilg: Hunting hill   NJ 1066 3521   Carn Sealgach

A prominent hill situated at the east of Advie parish. [OSNB]

Clais na Gaibhre: Goat hollow   NJ 1040 4203

A small hollow with two lochans in the north of the parish. The burn flows from only one of the two lochans. [OSNB]

Clash Tau: 1804

Coire Buidhe: Yellow hollow   NJ 0901 3845   Corr Buie 1804

A small hollow on the west side of Carn Eag, from which flows a small burn of the same name. [OSNB]

Corbuie Shieling: 1804   NJ 0903 3793

Corr na Larig: 1812   Corrie of the pass   NJ 0772 4043

Creag a'Bharrain: Hill of the sharp summit   NJ 1010 3505   Craig Varran (The Baron's Hill) 1804

A prominent hill over which the former county boundary crossed and situated about one mile to the west of Knockanbuie farmhouse. [OSNB] Also noted as the Baron's Hill which could be connected to the Regality Court and the Baron Baillies that were appointed. There was one for the Tulchan area dispensing justice.

Creag a' Phigidh: Crag of the jar or the robin   NJ 0872 3724

A hill on the east side of Geal Charn and divided from it by a small stream called Caochan Suil Dubh. It received its name from the story that a jar, being found upon the hill containing certain articles, but what they were nobody knows. [OSNB]

Cuchan ichk Gillie Chere: 1804   Burn of the left handed boy NJ 0833 3605

Culdorachmore and Sithean

Cuchan a Shalavack: 1812

Cuchan na Cruve: 1812   Burn of the tree

Cuchan-n-Ore: 1804   Burn of gold   NJ 1069 3657

Cuchan Taen: 1804   NJ 0929 3795

Cuchan Tuag: 1804   NJ 0863 3766

Culdorachbeg: The little dark back   NJ 1168 3620   Culdorrach Beg 1804, 1901

A former small but substantial farm house with offices, garden attached. [OSNB]

Culdorachmore: The large dark back   NJ 1080 3635   Culdorach More 1804

A former small farm house in Glen Tulchan, with offices, garden attached. [OSNB]

Cul Dorcha: The dark back   NJ 1045 3586

A small hill feature a little east of Carn Feurach nan Each. [OSNB]

Culdrein: The back of thorns   1851, 1901   NJ 1169 3556 Culdryoin 1804

A small farmstead and dwelling house of one storey in good repair. [OSNB]

Fields: Spartan, Gortan beg, Gortan more, Old Chaple. 1804

Culfoichbeg: Little nook of the cup shaped hollow   NJ 1154 3294 Littill Culquyhe 1611, Culquoichbeg 1767, Easter Culquoich beg 1802, Culfoichbegg 1851

A farmhouse one storey high with numerous offices attached, the whole slated and in excellent condition. [OSNB]

Fields: Lack More, Stau n Doul, The Dale, Tor Garrow, Easter Haugh. 1767

Fields: Braes, Ellan Riach, Cretan Yellan, Culfoichbeg, Haugh of Easter Culquoich, Bruntlands, Black Hillocks, Haugh of Black Hillocks. 1802

Wester Culquoich Begg: NJ 1150 3256

Fields: Dry Leys, Haugh of Culquoich Begg, The Braes. 1802

Culfoichmore: 1851   Large nook of the cup shaped hollow   NJ 0880 3227   Meikle Culquych 1611

A farm steading and dwelling house, one storey high, thatched and in good repair. [OSNB]

Fields: Lack na Toch, Bual a Gorum, Peol Torron Du, Auch na Carn, Torran na ha, Tor n Ailen, Cuil n Torran, Dall u Cruy, Ochku Ty Vore, Bual a Cloigh, Dalu Fat, Lach n Biea. 1810

Dalchroy: NJ 1409 3583   Delchroy 1804, Dalchroy 1901
Fields: Delna Aun, Isle of Delchroy, Laggan Riach 1804
A thatched farm house having outhouses etc attached. The dwelling house and one out house are in a state of ruins. [OSNB]

Dalchroy Lodge: NJ 1289 3563   Dalchroy House, Tulchan Lodge
Now known as Tulchan Lodge. The original house was built in 1789 as a Seafield family residence for shooting and fishing. Following a fire it was rebuilt and in 1938 changed the name to Tulchan Lodge.

Dalguish: 1804   Pine tree dale or meadow   NJ 1358 3803
A ruined farm house and outbuildings.

Delyorn: Field of barley   NJ 1164 3637
A small but substantial farm house with offices attached. [OSNB]
Field: Boul Bain 1804

Dir Lea: 1810   The grey grove   NJ 0959 3320   Derrylean
improvement 1767

Dubh-allt Beag: 1804   Little black burn   NJ 0859 3919
A burn at the head of Glen Tulchan. It rises on the Larig Hill and after a short run flows into the Dubh-Allt-Mor.

Dubh-allt Mor: 1804   Big black burn   NJ 0841 3923
A burn in Glen Tulchan which rises on the west side of the Larig Hill and flowing southward for about a mile, its waters join with those of other streams and forms the Burn of Tulchan.

Dugal's Wells: 1804   NJ 116 364

Durmore: 1804   Large grove NJ 118 363

Derry Lettoch: 1802   Half davoch grove NJ 1002 3335
Fields: Bruntland, Head of the Derry. 1802

Fouran-a-Glen: 1810   Spring of the glen   NJ 0868 3272

Furan-na-Chaal: 1804 NJ 086 384

Gallow Hill: see Carn na Croiche

Geal Charn: White or bright hill   NJ 0762 3696   Gyall Charn
1804
A high heather covered hill on the north side of Allt Lonn Mor and

west of Creig Phigeidh. [OSNB] On earlier maps the higher summit of Carn an Fhuarain Mhoir is called Geal Charn. Perhaps renamed to avoid confusion with the other Geal Charn, on the other side of Glen Tulchan.

Geal Charn: White or bright hill   NJ 1143 3793   Gyall Charn 1804

The highest ground in the north part of the parish of Advie and stands between the Burn of Tulchan, Carn Eag and the Gallow Hill. [OSNB] Conspicuous with its grass covered western slopes.

Glaichk Uaran Te-lich: 1810   NJ 0866 3243

Glen Brachk: 1775   Brindled Glen   NJ 0752 4111

Appears on only one map for the glen where the Allt Dearg flows.

Glen Gheallaidh: Glen of the promise or brightness, clear   NJ 1392 3789

The glen through which Allt Gheallaidh flows. It is about six miles long and from one to two miles in breadth. [OSNB]

Glenmore Loch: Large glen loch   NJ 0877 3391

A modern construction used for fishing by Tulchan Estate. The former farm of Luachar is submerged beneath it.

Glenmore Plantation: NJ 1013 3379

Glen Tulchan: Glen of little hillocks   NJ 0993 3686

A small glen through which flows the Burn of Tulchan. It is about three to four miles long by about one in breadth. [OSNB]

Hill of Dalchroy: NJ 1342 3624   Hill of Delchroy 1804

A prominent hill now covered in woodland overlooking the River Spey. To the north of Tulchan Lodge. [OSNB]

Knockanbuie: 1804   Little yellow hill   NJ 1169 3511 Cnockanbuie

A farmhouse one storey high with attics, also offices attached, the whole thatched and in good repair. [OSNB]

Fields: Lagheap, The Daldu, Haugh Ground, Wells called Clochdu, Reina Carn, Bruachanash. 1770

Fileds: Bruch-n-Aun 1804

Knocktulchan   Tulchan hill, hill of the little green hillocks   NJ 1182 3593   Knock Tulchen 1804

A substantial farm house with offices, garden etc attached. [OSNB]

Fields: Bruch-n-Aun, Auch Croum 1804

Mill of Knocktulchan: NJ 1192 7614   Mill of Tulchen 1804

A corn and saw mill on the west bank of the Burn of Tulchan. It consists of a stone building flanked on both sides by wooden buildings. [OSNB]

Lackanour: 1804   Little dun coloured hollow   NJ 1064 3561

Laglia: 1767   Grey hollow   NJ 0979 3262

Fields: Loch Gorum, Blae How, Lang Gavel, Ach Buie, Face Field, Stoney Fold, Bruntlands. 1802

Laggan Maisley: 1812   NJ 0637 3859

A hollow near the Black Loch.

Larig Hill: The hill pass   NJ 0868 4022   Hill of Larig 1775, The Larig 1812

At the head of Glen Tulchan on the former boundary between the counties of Inverness-shire and Moray and between the districts of Cromdale and Advie. [OSNB]

Croft of Lettoch: 1851   Half davoch

Easter Lettoch: 1767   Half davoch   NJ 1011 3286   Lettauche 1611

A farmhouse, one storey high with offices attached, thatched and in fair repair. [OSNB]

Fields: Town of Easter Lettoch, The Tron Well, Blackfold, Dow Hollow, New Waird, Mickle Back, Chappel Croft. 1802

Coul na ha. 1810

Wester Lettoch: 1767   Half davoch   NJ 0994 3271

A farmhouse and out offices one storey high, partly thatched and partly slated, in good repair. [OSNB]

Fields: Yard field, Breest, Mas More, Lagmore croft, croft of Lettoch, Laggan Calder, Seram Block. 1802

Fields: Bual du, Rue n leish, Auch Meinach, Dall u Du, Crait, Lack n

Caulten, Crait n Dollar, Neimer Vore. 1810

Linavaich: 1804   Enclosure of the byre   NJ 0947 3684

Loch Mhadadh: Wolf loch   NJ 1299 3721

A small marshy spot, barely a loch, on the north side of the Gallow Hill. It derives its name as it was once believed to be a haunt of wolves. [OSNB]

Luachar: 1810   Place of rushes   NJ 0874 3389

A former farm now submerged under Glenmore Loch

Polcreach: Pool of clay   NJ 1438 3662   Polcreach 1804, Poul-Creach 1851

A small farm steading of one storey in good repair, situated on the north side of the River Spey and about three quarters of a mile west of Fanmore. [OSNB]

Puchkan Diarn: 1804   or Laird's Bught   NJ 1030 3687

Site of old shieling.

Rie Uan: 1804   Lamb shieling   NJ 0846 3818

A former shieling, the site is now used by Tulchan Estate for a shooting hut.

Field: Ridalchaple   The horse shieling or slope

Scorgu: 1804   Pointed rock of the wind   NJ 117 366

Shihan Bea: 1804   Birch tree fairy hill   NJ 093 377

Shihan-n-Luie: 1804   Fairy hill of the calf   NJ 118 363

Shihan of Culdorrachmore: 1804   Fairy hill of the large dark back NJ 1076 3648

Sidhean Cul Grianain: Fairy hillock at the back of a sunny spot NJ 1131 3945   Shihan of Culagrinan 1804

A small knoll on the side of Allt Gheallaidh. [OSNB] This is one of the many hillocks in Tulchan, believed to be the home of fairies.

Sidhean Cul Grianain Shieling: NJ 112 394

Sithean Sron na Saobhaidhe: NJ 1053 3702   Fairy hillock at the nose or promontory of the fox's den.

A small hill between the forks of Caochan Sron na Saobhaidh and the Burn of Tulchan. One of several hillocks in Glen Tulchan thought to be the home of fairies.

Straan: Little strath   NJ 1223 3569   Stroin 1804

Applied to a crofter's dwelling house of one storey, thatched and in good repair with offices attached. [OSNB]

Fields: The Wester Haugh, Stron na faat, Easter Haugh, Torna-ha 1804

Easter Straan: NJ 1277 3557   Easter Strawn 1861

Applied to a dwelling house of one storey, thatched and in good repair, with a few acres of land attached to the property. [OSNB]

Stripe of Dirmore: Stream or ditch of the big grove   NJ 1215 3675

A small tributary of the Burn of Tulchan. It rises on the south side of Geal Charn and flows south for about a mile. [OSNB]

Stripe of Taurnac: Stream of pebbles   NJ 1292 3584

A small burn rising a little west of the hill Cairn na Croich, which following a southerly course of about three quarters of a mile joins the River Spey near Eilean na Muic. [OSNB]

Stron na Suvie: 1804   Nose or promontory of the fox   NJ 1026 3715

Stron na Suvie Shieling: 1804   NJ 1039 3706

Tom Farish: Watching hill   NJ 1262 3609   Toum Farrash 1804

A tract of rising ground, heavily wooded on the north side of the River Spey and occupying the space between the Spey, the burns of Tulchan and Tuarnac and the Gallow Hill. [OSNB]

Tom na Laimh: Hill of the hand   NJ 1080 3328   Toum na Laie 1810 [OSNB]

Toum na Heuler: 1810   Hill of the eagle   NJ 0923 3281

Not named on modern Ordnance Survey maps.

Tulchan: A green hillock

An area north of the River Spey with several farms in its lower reaches, rising through wooded area to open moorland.[OSNB]

Formerly part of the Seafield Estate, it is now famed for fishing and grouse shooting.

Tulchan Bridge: NJ 1216 3560

A bridge which crosses Tulchan Burn, situated a little west of the croft of Straan. [OSNB]

Tulchan Lodge (Old):   NJ 1119 3372

Tulchan Lodge (New):   NJ 1288 3563   Dalchroy House

Built in 1906 by George McCorquodale after original Dalchroy House was destroyed by fire. Changed name from Dalchroy House to Tulchan Lodge in 1938. Edward VII was a frequent visitor.

Tulchan Pool: NJ 1209 3540

A deep pool in the River Spey and famed for salmon fishing. Situated a little east of Spey bridge of Tulchan, now known as Bridge of Advie. [OSNB]

Bridge of Tulchanpool: NJ 1202 3533   Spey Bridge of Advie

The original wooden bridge was constructed in 1868 by subscription under the patronage of the Earl of Seafield and crossed the River Spey a little west of the Croft of Straan. New bridge now called Spey Bridge of Advie. [OSNB]

WALKS

1: Lettoch to Carn an Fhradhairc

On the B9102 just past Easter Lettoch, a hill track on Tulchan estate skirts the eastern flank of Carn na Doire to Glenmore Loch. The loch stocked with brown trout, is a man-made reservoir, now with added fishing facilities for the estate guests. Before reaching the loch, the track branches to the right, heading north-east and steadily climbs anti clockwise to Bad an Each (clump of the horse 469m,1538 ft). The view over the River Spey starts to open up and just a little further the top of the aptly named Carn an Fhradhairc (hill of the good view 503m, 1650 ft) is reached. The track can be followed a little further towards the trig point on the slightly higher Carn na Loine (hill of the marsh 549m, 1801ft) and then drop down towards the marshy area, where the Allt Luchair (burn of rushes) rises. Beyond this, the return track can be joined north of Tom Mor, with the transmitter pylon on the summit. Follow the track just below the summit ridge, overlooking Glenmore Loch and the rocky southern, scree slope of Carn Fhradhairc back to the junction and route down to the main road.

2: Tulchan Circuit

Just beyond the wooden bridge over the Tulchan Burn and the cottages at Straan, there's an entrance to Tulchan on the left hand side. A circular walk returning to the same location can be made in either direction. Going through the right handside gate, the track rises through Straan Wood and the Hill of Dalchroy, overlooking Tulchan Lodge and the River Spey below.

Tulchan Lodge was originally called Dalchroy and built in 1789 as a residence for hunting and shooting. It proved popular with the proprietor, the 7th Earl of Seafield and Sir Phillip Sassoon. The latter, financial advisor to Edward VII frequently visited with the king, especially for the grouse season. The first lodge was destroyed by fire, and the current structure was built by George McCorquodale in 1906. Renamed Tulchan Lodge in 1938, it was sold after the death of the Countess of Seafield in 1969. The current owner is Russian billionaire, Yuri Shefler.

Soon onto the open hill above Glen Tulchan, the track continues to climb towards the summit of Geal Charn (white hill 456m, 1496ft) and its grassy western flank, standing out among the heather clad hills. Before the summit, a branch of the track leads right and after a short walk reveals Loch Mhadadh (loch of the wolf). Not so much a loch, rather a green patch where a burn of the same name rises.

Having reached the summit of Geal Charn, the track stretches out along the broad ridge running parallel to the Tulchan Burn below, and to the highest point on the walk, Carn na-Eige (hill of the notch 513m,1683 ft). The track now descends towards the glen where a number of streams join to form the infant Tulchan Burn. Beyond the confluence rises Larig Hill and an old route that descended to the Allt Dearg and Ourack Burn, where it meets with the Via Regia onwards into the lowlands of Moray.

Crossing the Tulchan Burn by a ford, a shooting hut, ruins and grassy knolls are all that remain of the former shieling of Ruighe Uain (lamb shieling). The track now heads downstream through pockets of pine wood and crossing the numerous burns coming off the hill. Here and there are further piles of stones, hidden among the heather, remains of former shielings: Corbuie, Shihan Bea, Cuchan na Heulre, Linaveach and Balnruich. On the right side of the track appears a large standing stone, standing guard with another round one perched on top. Surely of some significance, they appear of great antiquity, perhaps marking a boundary or a display of strength? No name could be found for the structure and on further enquiring alas, it appears to have been erected about forty years ago.

The people who lived and worked in the glen were not alone. Glen Tulchan has the highest number of place names associated with fairies in the whole parish. Partly as a result of the last ice age, deposits of debris formed moraines on the glen floor. Not hard to spot, looking like inverted Christmas puddings or shian (fairy hillocks), were the perfect residence for the little people: Shian Bea (fairy hill of the birch tree), Shihan-n-Luie (fairy hill of the calf) and Sithean Sron na Saobhaidhe (fairy hill of the fox's nose, promontory).

The track now begins to diverge from the burn to Culdarochmore with its rusty corrugated iron roof, nestling below its own Shihan of Culdorachmore, (fairy hill of the large dark back). Continue past the fields, avoiding Knocktulchan, ford the Tulchan Burn for the final time and shortly return to the start.

Standing Stone, Tulchan

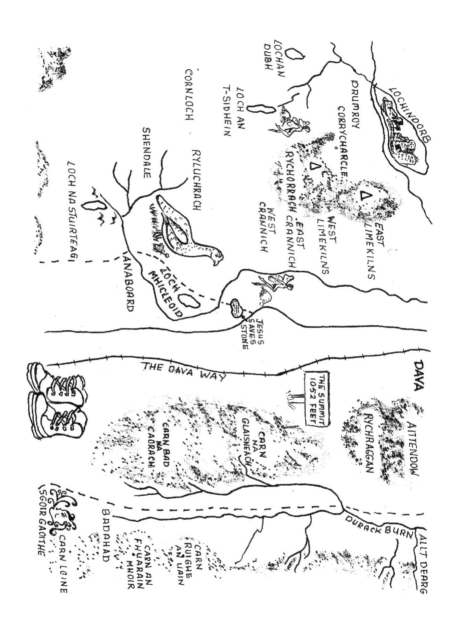

LOCHAN DUBH

LOCH AN T-SIDHEIN

CORNLOCH

SHENDALE

RYLUCHRACH

LOCH NA STUIRTEAG

LANABOARD

LOCH MHICLEOID

DRUMROY

CORRYCHARCLE

RYCHORRACH

WEST CRANNICH

EAST CRANNICH

WEST LIMEKILNS

EAST LIMEKILNS

LOCHINDORB

JESUS SAVES STONE

THE DAVA WAY

THE SUMMIT 1052 FEET

DAVA

RYCHRAGGAN

AITTENDOW

CARN BAD NA CAORACH

CARN NA GLAISNEACH

DURACK BURN

AULT DEARG

SGOIR GAOTHE

CARN LOINE

BADDHAD

CARN AN FHUARAIN MHOIR

CARN RUIGHE AN UAIN

140

CHAPTER 6

The Dava Moor

A Fouran More 1809: The large spring NH 965 307

Aittendow: Black Juniper NJ 0276 3913 Aiten du Improvement 1775, Aighten Du1810

A small farmhouse having suitable offices attached, one storey high, thatched and in bad condition. [OSNB]

The Aittendow shown on current Ordnance Survey maps is on the site of Ruighsean (Reuain). The original Aittendow was further east on the same brow of the hill, with substantial ruins still surviving.

Allt a'Choire Odhair Bhig: Burn of the small dun hollow NH 9533 3213

A burn rising near to Loch Ruigh a'Bhuair and flowing in a north eastern course, until it joins Glentarroch Burn, a short distance south of Glentarroch farm house. [OSNB]

Allt Bad a'Ghad: Burn of the cluster of twisted twigs NJ 0413 3777

A very small burn rising on the east side of Blar an Sgoir Ghaothaich and forms with Allt Bad na Caorach the burn known as Allt Bad na Ciob. [OSNB]

Allt Bad a'Ghlussaid: Burn of the moving clump, unstable ground NJ 0461 3877

A small burn rising east of Badnagad Cottage, flowing in a northern direction and in conjunction with Allt Bog na Cioba, form the source of Ourack Burn. [OSNB]

Allt Bad na Caorach: Burn of the sheep clump NJ 0331 3712 Ault Bad Chuir 1810, Cairn Kilickeer

A small burn rising near the watershed at Cree Dearg, flowing northerly for upwards of two miles, where it unites with Allt Bog na Cioba. [OSNB]

Allt Bog na Cioba: Burn of the mountain grass bog NJ 0368 3849 see Allt Bog na Fiodhaig Burn of the Bird Cherry bog, Bog n Figack 1810

A burn formed by the union of Allt Bad na Caorach and Allt Bad na Gad and joining the Ourack Burn, a few hundred yards south of Ourack. Name that appears on modern Ordnance Survey maps.

Allt Bog na Fiodhaig: Burn of the Bird Cherry bog   NJ 0368 3849   Bog n Figack 1810

Older name on maps for Allt Bog na Cioba [OSNB]

Allt Coire na Burralaich: Burn of the hollow of lamentation, crying, wailing NJ 0071 3246 Ault Corry Waulich 1809, Allt Coire Buidhe

A small burn which rises in Coire na Burralaich, flows in a northern direction and joins Allt Loch na Stuirgaige close to its junction with Anaboard Burn. [OSNB] On modern maps is now called Allt Coire Buidhe.

Allt Loch an t-Sithein: Stream of the fairies knoll loch   NH 9711 3274   Allt Loch an t-Sidhein, Ault na Calich 1809

A burn flowing out of Loch an t-Sithein. It runs in a north westerly direction about 1 mile and joins Feith a'Mhor-Fhir near the junction of Glentarroch Burn. [OSNB] An Calich is the old woman or witch. A character well known in Celtic mythology. Note the burn is close to a shian or fairy hill.

Allt Loch na Stuirgaige: Burn of the black headed gull loch   NJ 0036 3321   Allt Loch na Stuirteag

A small stream rising from the moor near Loch na Stuirgaige, running north easterly into Anaboard Burn, a few hundred yards south of Anaboard. [OSNB]

Allt na Ceardaich: Burn of the smithy   NJ 0109 3778

A burn rising a little to the south of the farm of Aittendow, running south westerly until quite close to the former Highland line, thence turning northwards and flowing to Dava where it flows into Annabord Burn. [OSNB]

Allt Suileagach: Stream full of bubbles   NH 9752 3557   Ault Sulak 1809,

A small burn having its source south east of Lochindorb and flowing in a north easterly direction until it enters Loch an Dorb, north of Lochindorb Lodge. [OSNB]

Anaboard: NJ 0076 3359   Ain-na-Bord 1804, Anabord 1841,

Annabord 1851, Achnabord, Achnaboard post 1805, Aan a Board 1807

A small farmhouse: cot house and offices, all one storey high, thatched and in bad condition. [OSNB]

Anaboard Burn: NJ 0009 3353   Burn of Achnaboard

A large burn rising from a moor westward of Loch na Stuirgaige. Its course is northerly and about six miles in extent. It joins the Dorback Burn at Dava. [OSNB]

Ault na Calich: 1809   Burn of the old woman or witch   NH 9656 3303   All Loch an t-Sithein

An older name for Allt Loch an t-Sithein. This stretch of the burn is close to the shian or fairy hill.

Ault Tarsin: 1812   NJ 0521 3799 The crossways burn

Aultarsen Improvement: 1775 NJ 04620 38902   Croft Tarsin 1812

Badahad: NJ 0478 3730   Badghatt improvement 1767

Baddanyoir improvement: 1775 Small grass clump   NJ 033 400 Badden Voir 1812, Baddevoir 1862

Badinluaskin: NJ 052 376   1767 improvement, Badden Luiskan 1812

Bad na Caorach: Clump of the sheep   NJ 0292 3670   Bad Chuir 1810

A grassy part on Carn Clais an Eich. [OSNB]

Badnagad Cottage: NJ 0479 3730

A small dwelling house formerly occupied by a gamekeeper. [OSNB]

Bad a Gual: 1809   Clump of coal   NH 9824 3074

A hard black peat.

Bad Chat: 1809   Cat Clump   NH9987 3329

Blaar Bad a Gat: 1810   Moss of the cluster of twisted twigs   NJ 042 372

Blaar Clash na Cluanach: 1809 Moss of the hollow of pasture NH 9850 3292

Blaar Dir Lea: 1810   Moss of the grey grove   NJ 032 343

Blaar Dreim Guish: 1810   Moss of the pine ridge   NJ 0131 3705

Blaar Fae Vorrer: 1809   Moss of the bog stream of the great man NH 9623 3288

Blaar Fouran More: 1809   Moss of the big spring   NH 9624 3148

Blaar More: 1809   Big moss   NH 9597 3343

Blair Glen Gour: 1809   Moss of the goat glen   NH 9837 3339

Blair na Calich: 1809   Moss of the old woman or witch   NH 9662 3320

Blair n Rue Luecharoch: 1809   Moss of the shieling of rushes   NH 9916 3292

Blar an Sgoir Ghaothaidh: Moss of the windy point   NJ 0434 3677   Blar an Sgoir Gaoithe

An extensive tract of moss extending a mile north west of Huntly's Cave. [OSNB]

Blar Creag a'Bheithe: Moss of the birch craig   NJ 0141 3306

A large moor extending for a mile and a half between Carn Luig and Loch na Cloich Mhuilinn. It was formerly extensively used as a peat moss by the inhabitants of Grantown. [OSNB]

Bridge of Dava: NJ 0046 3898   Bridge of Dorback, Paul's Bridge

A single stone bridge across the Dorback Burn erected around 1755 during the construction of the military road from Old Spey Bridge to Fort George. [OSNB]

Caar More Ruenechkera: 1809   Large ridge of the shieling stock pen   NH 9825 3173

Cairn a Gillie Vure: 1809   Hill of the cattle boy, herdsman   NH 9344 3264

Cairn Bad Na Caorach: Hill of the sheep clump   NJ 0317 3546 Carn Bad Chuir 1810 [OSNB]

Cairn Duna Goint: 1809   NH 9888 3091

Cairnloch: The hill of the loch, corrie of the loch   NH 9712 3130 Corr n Loch 1809, Corrinloch 1761, Coranloch 1841, Cornloch 1851.

A farmhouse and out offices, one storey high thatched and in good repair. [OSNB]

On earlier maps occurs as Cornloch, the corrie of the loch.

Cairn na Shaundale: 1809   Hill of the old field   NH 9912 3120

Caochan a'Bhric: Trout stream   NH 9739 3150   Caochan Nam Breac [OSNB]

Caochan Ban: White stream   NH 9606 3102

A small burn rising from the northern side of Cam Sgriob and flowing in a north westerly direction until it joins Feith a Mhor. [OSNB]

Caochan Dorch: Dark stream   NH 9605 3491   Cuchan Dorach 1809

A small burn which rises about a mile to the north of Glentarroch farm house and running eastwards, falling into the southern end of Lochindorb. [OSNB]

Caochan Neachdarach: The neutral burn   NH 9466 3214 [OSNB]

Caochan Ruadh: Red burn   NJ 0060 3445

A small stream rising a short distance south of the farm of Rychorrach and falling into Anaboard Burn at Uig. [OSNB]

Carn a Feachan Du: 1810   NJ 0425 3615

Carn Aighteen Du: 1810   Hill of the black juniper   NJ 0270 3943 Carn an Achaidh Dhuibh, Carn Ruigh Thuim

On 1st edition Ordnance Survey map it's called Carn an Achaidh Dhuibh, but on modern OS maps been incorrectly called Carn Ruigh Thuim.

Carn an Druim Ruaidh: Hill of the red ridge   NH 9708 3426   Dreim Ruay 1809,

A small hill about half a mile north of Drumroy. [OSNB]

Carn an Fhuarain Mhoir: The large spring hill   NJ 0664 3692 [OSNB]

Carn Bad a'Ghad: Hill of the cluster of twisted twigs   NJ 0383 3666 Cairn Bad a Gat 1810,

Carn Bad nan Gad

A small oval hill lying midway between Allt Bad nan Gad and in a direct line between Bad na Caorach and Blar Sgoir Ghaothaich. [OSNB]

Carn Biorach: The sharp pointed hill   NJ 0175 3904 [OSNB]

On modern Ordnance Survey maps this summit now has no name and the name has been given to its neighbour that was previously Carn Ruigh Uaine.

Carn Claish an Eich: Hill of the horse hollow   NJ 0224 3605 Glassinoch Hill 1724, Carn Glashnich, 1810, Carn na Glaisneach

A large round hill, lying a mile and a half south east of Dava Station. [OSNB]. Donald Roy McGrigor in Tiriebeg stated on a perambulation of this hill 21, 22 Oct 1724, there were shielings on skirts of this hill.

Carn Cruinn: Round hill   NH 9752 3101   Craggan Cruin 1809

A prominent round rocky hill south east of Cairnloch. [OSNB]

Carn na h-Ath-aoil: Hill of the limekiln   NH 9899 3553   Cairn a ha ual 1809, Na Hril Pont? Cairn na Ail Roy

A hill west of Uig and northwest of Rychorrach. [OSNB]

Carn na Leitire: Hill of the steep shelving ground or broad slope NH 9339 3062

Situated to the east side of Cnoc an Lamhaich beside the main road. [OSNB]

Carn nan Clach Garbha: Hill of the rough stones   NH 9452 3469 Cairn Glaichk Garrie 1809

A low hill on a short range which formed the boundary between the County of Nairn and Inverness and about 1 ½ miles south west of Lochindorb. [OSNB]

Carn nan Gabhar: Hill of the goats   NH 9788 3336   Cairn a Glen Gour 1809, [OSNB]

Carn Ruighe an Uain: Hill of the lamb shieling   NJ 0190 3905

A conspicuous hill situated on the former parish and county boundary and on the lands of the Right Hon the Earl of Seafield and the Earl of Moray. [OSNB]

Modern Ordnance Survey maps have given this name to what was previously called Carn Aighteen Du. The original Carn Ruighe an Uain is the hill now called Carn Biorach. This grid reference is for the original hill of that name.

Carn Rue Craggan: 1810   Hill of the rocky shieling or slope   NJ

0183 3827

Carn Ruigh na Caorach: Hill of the sheep shieling or hill of the steep shieling   NH 9899 3467   Cairn Rue Corroch 1809, Carn Ruigh Chorrach.

Early maps suggest it could be steep (corrach) shieling rather sheep (caorach)

A heathy pasture hill a mile east of Corrycharcle. [OSNB]

Carn Ruigh Thuim: Hill of the lamb shieling   NJ 0191 3905   Carn Ruigh Uaine, Carn Rue Huin, 1810 [OSNB]

Modern Ordnance Survey maps now incorrectly give this name to Carn Aighteen Du.

Carr Mor: Large mossy place   NJ 0131 3728

A mossy place extending ½ a mile along the east side of the former Highland line, a mile south of Dava Station. [OSNB]

Carr Mor: Large morass, large peat moss   NH 9825 3174   Caar More Rue Nechkera 1809

A large peat moss situated about quarter of a mile east of Loch an t-Sithein. [OSNB]

Clach Glass: 1812   Grey stone   NJ 0460 3889

A large stone in the improvement field upstream from the Ourack.

Clais an Eich: Horse hollow   NJ 0230 3734   Glaisneach, Glashnich 1810

A hollow lying at the north base of Carn Clais an Eich. [OSNB]

Clash Doin: 1809   Brown or bronze coloured hollow   NH 972 346

Clash na Cluanach: 1809   Hollow of pasture   NH 9861 3328

Cnoc an Lamhaich: Knoll of the casting with hands   NH 9304 3094

A small but very conspicuous hill situated a short distance to the east of Carn Allt Laoigh. [OSNB]

Cnocan Buidhe: 1809   Yellow hillock

Corr Our Bog: 1809   Little dun coloured corrie   NH 9511 3145

Corr Our More: 1809   Large dun coloured corrie   NH 9458 3056

Coire na Burralaich: Hollow of lamentation, crying, wailing   NJ 0098 3179   Corry Verulich 1809, Corrie Buidhe.

Hollow at the north side of Creag Liath, out of which a stream of the same name runs. [OSNB]

On current Ordnance Survey maps now called Coire Buidhe.

Corrycharcle: Hollow of the hoop, round hollow   NH 9781 3474 Korichertil (Pont), Coir Chearteil 1793, Corrycharckle improvement 1808, Corry Charkle, 1809, Corcharcle 1841, Corchearcle 1851, Corycharkle 1871

A farm steading, dwelling house and offices one storey high, thatched and in middling repair. [OSNB] Corrieharkill, the hill has several shieling's on the skirts of it 1724.

Cow & Calf: 1724   NJ 0439 3975

One large and one smaller boulder a few meters apart, partly now hidden by heather.

Craggan Baddandeoig: 1809   NH 9682 3206

Craggan Cara: 1809   NH 9752 3101

Craggan na Meaun: 1809   Little rocks of the kids (goats)   NH 9679 3048

Craggan Narroch: 1809   Little rocks of the snake, serpent   NH 9544 3111

Craig Tiribeg: Rock of the small land or rock of the small grove NH 9855 3600   Tyrbeg (Roy), Slauchk Bannauk 1809

A prominent hill situated at the north western end of Lochindorb. [OSNB]

Easter Crannich: Place of the trees   NJ 0032 3470   Easter Crannich improvement 1808, Easter Crannach 1809, Easter Crannach 1861

A small farm steading having suitable offices attached, all in bad repair. [OSNB]

Fields: Toumvaich, Stau Chat, Stau na ha, Crait Nathach. 1809

Wester Crannich: NH 9992 3433   Wester Crannich Improvement 1808, Crannichen 1841, Wester Crannach 1861, Crannich 1901,

A small farmhouse with suitable offices, one storey high and in bad condition. [OSNB]

Shianacranich: Fairy hill of the trees   NJ 0083 3532   Shien Cran 1724, Shian a Craunich 1807

Creag a'Ghiuthais: Rock of the pine tree   NH 9490 3188   [OSNB]

Creagan na h-Othaisge: Small crag of the sheep (one year old ewe)   NH 9857 3117

A small hill near Carr Mor and Shendale. [OSNB]

Cuchan Du: Black or dark burn 1812   NJ 0497 4033

Dava: 1810   Deer or ox ford   NJ 0038 383   Davah, Dava Crofts 1808 rental [OSNB]

Dava Inn: 1851   NJ 0038 3835   Dava Farm 1901

A roadside inn with farm steading attached, dwelling house and out offices, one storey high, thatched and in middling repair. [OSNB]

Dava Post Office: NJ 0083 3893

A branch office attached to the Dava Station for the convenience of people residing in the locality. There is one arrival and one despatch daily. [OSNB]

Dava School: NJ 0039 3851

Dava School Plantation: NJ 0065 3875

Dava Shieling:

Not located, mentioned briefly in records.

Dava Station: NJ 0082 3893

A side station on the Highland Railway with post office attached-one arrival and despatch daily. [OSNB] Open from 1864 to 1965.

Dava Summit: NJ 0106 3665   The Summit 1901

A house near the summit of the old railway line in 1901 census. The railway summit is 320m (1052 ft) above sea level.

Dir Lea: 1810   Grey grove   NJ 029 343

An old enclosure.

Dorback Burn: Small fish burn   NH 9774 3755   The Dorback Roy, Ault Dorback 1807 [OSNB]

Dreim du Lochan Dhian: Ridge of the fairy hill loch 1809   NH 9766 3257

Dreim du Rue n Dhian: Ridge of the fairy hill shieling 1809   NH 9672 3178

Drumguish: Ridge of the pine tree   NJ 0063 3734   Drumghuish improvement 1807, Dreim Guish 1809, Drimush 1841, Drumgush 1851, Drumguish 1901

This place consists of a farm dwelling, steading and offices all one storey high, thatched and in fair condition. [OSNB]

Drumroy: The ruddy brown ridge   NH 9681 3380   Drum Roy 1724, Dreim Ruay 1809, Druimroy 1851

A farm steading, dwelling house and offices, one storey high thatched and in middling repair. [OSNB]

Field: Crait 1809

Ehg an Dhiam: 1809   The fairy hill notch or gap   NH 9873 3426

Fae Muluch: 1809   Bog stream of the top, summit   NH 9961 3288 Feith Tharsuinn

Older name was Feith Tharsuinn, the crossways bog stream.

Fae Vaddan: Bog stream of the little clumps   NJ 0380 4042 Fae Vattan 1812

Feabain: 1761   White bog stream   NH 9944 3324   Fea Baan 1809

An old shieling.

Feith a'Chaoruin: Bog stream of the rowan tree   NJ 0371 4070 Fae Churn 1812

A small burn rising north of Aittendow and was the boundary for a mile between the parish of Edinkillie and this parish. [OSNB]

Feith a' Mhor-fhir: Morass, bog stream of the great man   NH 9590 3217   Fea Vorrir or the Earl's Myre 1724, Fae Vorrer 1809

A hill burn rising about a mile and a half to the south of Glentarroch house and having a northern course for about two and half miles, where it joins the Glentarroch Burn near to where that stream flows into Lochindorb. [OSNB]

Feith Bhan: White small stream or moss   NJ 0078 3574

A tributary of Anaboard Burn, it rises in a moss east of Sithean an Aiteil, flows into Loch an Eilean on the south east side, leaves it on the opposite side, where it is spanned by a bridge on the former County Road and pursues the same course until it flows into Anaboard Burn. [OSNB]

Feith Tharsuinn: Crossways bog stream   NJ 0159 3739   Feith Mullach   [OSNB]

On modern maps now called Feith Mullach.

Dorch an Uaran: 1809   Dark spring   NH 9995 3129

Fuarn Phatrick: Peter's Well 1724   NJ 006 377

Glaichk Garrie: 1809   Rough hollow   NH 9370 3317

Glaichk na Criu Fearn: 1809   Hollow of the alder tree   NH 9500 3371

Glaisneach: 1810   Horse hollow   NJ 023 373

An old enclosure surrounded in juniper.

Glengour: Goat Glen   NH 9816 3335   Glengour 1806, Glen Gour 1809, Glengower 1841

A farm steading, partly in ruins, dwelling house and offices, one storey high, thatched and in bad repair. [OSNB]

Field names: Marlach More, Rue Eulay, Crait Du 1809

House of Glengour: NH 9885 3368

Glentarroch: NH 9519 3291   Glentarrach 1861, Glen Tearroch 1809, Glentearach 1807 rental, Low Glentearach Roy

This name is applied to a farm house, one storey high with stabling byres etc attached, the whole thatched and in fair repair. [OSNB]

Glentarroch Burn: NH 9559 3350   Glentorrach Roy,

A small burn rising about one mile to the west of Glentarroch farm and flowing in a north east course until it flows into Lochindorb. [OSNB]

Heatherbell: 1901   NJ 0086 3648

Jesus Saves Stone: NJ 0100 3505

Knockan Durick: 1809   NH 9802 3417

Larich Vore: 1809   Big slope   NH 9688 3551

Easter Limekilns: NH 9925 3690   Limekills Roy, Easter Lime Kiln 1808, Easter Limekilns 1851,   East Lime Kilns 1871,

Wester Limekilns: NH 9970 3593   Lymekillns 1724, Wester Lymekiln 1793, Wester Lime Kiln 1809, Limekilns 1841, West Lime Kilns 1871

This name is applied to a farmhouse, steading and out houses, all of which are one storey, thatched and in bad condition. [OSNB] In 1676 horses were stolen from Ballintomb and found at the shieling of Limekilns, Lochindorb.

Lochan a'Chaorainn: Lochan of the rowan tree   NJ 0393 4080 Lochuchk ne Voir 1775, Lochick ill Voir 1812

A small lochan over the centre of which passed the former boundary between this and the parish of Edinkillie. [OSNB]

Lochan Dubh: Black little loch   NH 9567 3272   Lochandow Roy [OSNB]

Loch an Dunain: Loch of the knoll   NJ 0088 3604

A small loch lying between Loch an Eilean and the former Highland line. [OSNB]

Loch an t-Sithein: Loch of the fairy knoll   NH 9729 3221 Lochantian Roy, Lochan Dhian 1809 Loch an t-Sidhein

A small loch situated about two miles south of Lochindorb. [OSNB]

Loch Ille Mhor: Loch of the big ghille   NH 9346 3199

Lochnellan: Loch of the Island   Lochnellan 1841, Lochanellan 1901

A farm dwelling having suitable offices attached, situated near the loch from which it derives its name. [OSNB]

Lochan Eilean: Loch of the island   NJ 0066 3614   Loch Allan 1809

A small lochan situated on the moor south of Dava. [OSNB] The small island on the loch was known to float about the surface, driven by supernatural forces of local witches.

Loch Gillie Vure: 1809   Loch of the cattle boy, cow herd   NH 9349 3199

Now called Loch Ruigh a'Bhuair on modern maps.

Lochindorb: Loch of the small fish or stormy, wild loch   NH 9737 3604   Loch E Duirb Pont, Loch n Dorib 1724, Loch an Dorb Roy [OSNB]

Braes of Lochindorb: NH 9842 3573

Lochindorb Castle: NH 9745 3633

13th century castle built by the Comyns. Occupied by Edward I in 1303 and later home to Alexander Stewart, known as the 'Wolf of Badenoch'. Since 1456 been a ruin, when the Douglas family fell from power and the king ordered its destruction. [OSNB]

Lochindorb Lodge: NH 9691 3551   Lochindorb Shooting Lodge 1841, Lochin Dorb Lodge 1861,

A commodious house situated on the eastern shore of Lochan Dorb. It is two storeys high, slated and in good repair. Name written in accordance with estate documents viz-Lochindorb. [OSNB]

Lochindorb Gamekeeper's House: 1871   NH 9699 3539

Lochindorb Wood: NH 9728 3564

Loch Mhic Leoid: McLeod's Loch   NJ 0086 3470   Loch Cloed Roy, Loch Mcleod 1809

A loch situated east of Easter Crannich. [OSNB]

Loch na Cloiche-muilinn: Loch of the mill stone   NJ 0067 3437

A small circular lochan south of Crannich. [OSNB]

Lochnafeanag: Loch of the crow   NH 9973 3221   Roy, Loch na Stiartak 1809

Loch na Stuirgaige: Loch of the seagull (Black Headed Gull)   NJ 0016 3202

Lochnaskerry Roy, Loch na Stiartak 1809, Loch na Stuirteag

A small lochan partially covered with long grass situated quarter of a mile west of Coire na Burralaich. [OSNB] This is a local name given to the seagulls, which frequent the Highland lochs during the summer months.

Loch Ruigh a' Bhuair: Loch of the cattle shieling   NH 9349 3199 Loch Gillie Vure 1809

A small loch situated about one mile south west of Glentarroch farm house and close to the former county boundary. [OSNB]

Luachar Vaan: 1810   White rushes   NJ 034 380

Military Road: NJ 0121 3229

The road built in 1755 by Major Caulfeild from Old Spey Bridge to Fort George. [OSNB]

Millstone Ford: NH 9944 3864

A shallow ford on the Dorback Burn which crosses to Edinkillie parish. [OSNB]

Nechkera: 1809   Stock pen   NH 9459 3195

Ourack: Dun colour   NJ 0462 3972   Aurach Improvement 1775, Aurack, 1810

This name applies to a small dwelling house in miserable condition. It is occupied by a shepherd. [OSNB]   On the old road from Strathspey to Forres, 1775.

Ourack Burn: NJ 0459 3969   Aurack Burn 1724, Burn of Aurack 1812

A large burn formed by the confluence of Allt Bog na Ciob and Allt Bad a Ghluasaid. [OSNB]

Little Ourack: NJ 0485 4073

This place consists of a number of old ruins [OSNB]   Occupied in

1851 census.

Rebain: The white slope or shieling NH 9881 3370 Rue Baan 1809

Roman Road: see Via Regia

Rue Luchak: 1809 Mouse shieling NJ 0049 3304

Rue Sparden: 1810 Shieling of the hen roost NJ 021 355

An enclosure on Carn na Glaisneach.

Ruigh Sean: Old shieling NJ 0205 3881 Ryhuin 1808, Rue Huin 1810, Reuain 1851, Aittendow

A small farm steading now in ruins. [OSNB]

On older maps is Reuain, or lamb shieling. Current maps call it Aittendow. The original Aittendow was slightly further east and its ruins can still be seen.

Rychorrach: Hill of the steep sided shieling NH 9951 3433 Rhichorrhach 1801, Rycorrach improvement 1807, Rue Corroch 1809 Rycorrach 1841, Rychorach 1871

Applies to a small dwelling house having suitable offices attached. [OSNB] Rental linked with davoch of Dreggie.

Rychraggan: The stony slope or shieling NJ 01969 38032 Rue Craggan, 1810, Recraggan 1851,

A farm steading, dwelling house and out offices, one storey high, thatched and in middling repair. [OSNB]

Ryhuin: Lamb shieling NJ 0205 3881 Ryhuin 1808, Rue Huin 1810, Reuain 1851

Now appears as Ruigh Sean or old shieling.

Ryluachrach: Shieling of the rushes NH 9878 3270 Ryluachrach 1759, Rue Luocharoch 1809, Rue Luchak 1809

A farm steading, dwelling house and offices, one storey high, thatched and in bad repair. [OSNB]

Ryndian: Shieling of the fairy hill NH 9696 3262 Rue n Dhian 1809, Rhyndean 1841, Reghean 1851, Rygean 1861, Ryntian 1871,

A farm steading, one storey high, thatched and in bad repair, dwelling house attached. [OSNB]

Sassenachs Hut: 1871   NJ 0180 3322

Appears in 1871 census and later became the railway cottages at Huntly's Cave.

Sgor Gaothach: Windy rock   NJ 0523 3617

A prominent peak situated on the watershed, a short distance east of Huntly's Cave. [OSNB]

Shendale: Old meadow   NH 9869 3192   Shendale 1750, Improvement of Shendale 1786,   Shendale 1808, Shaundale 1809, Shendal 1841, Shandale 1851

A farm steading, dwelling house and offices, one storey high, thatched and in bad repair. [OSNB]

Shian: Fairy hill 1808   NH 9693 3302   Shian 1809

Sithean an Aiteil: The juniper fairy hill   NJ 0091 3510   Sidhean an Aiteil, Shian a Craunich 1810 [OSNB]

Earlier name, fairy hill of the trees.

A prominent hillock beside the main Grantown to Forres road. Current Ordnance Survey maps call it Sithean an Aiteil (juniper fairy hill) but for a long time on maps and usage was known as Shian a Crannich (fairy hill of the trees)

Slauchk Bannauk   1809   NH 9855 3600

Old name for Craig Tirebeg

The Summit: 1901

See Dava Summit.

Tiribeg;   The little land or little grove NH 9782 3628 Tiriebeg 1724, Tyrbeg Roy, Tirebeg 1808, Thiry Beg 1809, Tirbeg 1851,Tearbegg 1861 [OSNB]

Tiribeg Wood: NH 9844 3649

Tor Sloch Kanach: 1809   NH 9659 3244

Uig: The nook or solitary hollow   NJ 0053 3535   Shianaitten 1808, Uik 1809, Uike 1861, Uik 1871,

A small farm dwelling having suitable offices at hand, one storey high and in fair repair. [OSNB]

Via Regia: NJ 0457 3870   King's Highway   [OSNB]

A very old road once crossed the River Spey at Garbha Mhor and followed the current road to above Auchnagallin. It continues beyond there by Huntly's Cave and onto the Ourack. It was possibly a Via Regia or King's Road dating as far back as the 12th century, which linked Strathspey to Forres and Elgin in the medieval period. On some maps it is recorded as Roman, but there is no evidence for this and was the view of 19th century antiquarians.

Heatherbell

Walks

There are several routes that can be taken to explore this area. The estate has over recent years created more landrover roads and other hill and sheep tracks criss-cross the moor. Please respect the seasonal activities of the estate, especially during spring and autumn, when nesting birds and grouse shooting are active.

1: Lochindorb to Loch an t-Sidhean

From the A939 take the minor road from Dava junction to Lochindorb and drive along the loch shore, past the famous castle, to park just before the road turns to the right at the western end of the loch. Here on the left, a hill track leads to the abandoned farm of Drumroy and south across the western moorland of the Dava. A place which is often described as an isolated, empty, wild, wilderness and home to only grouse. Yet the numerous abandoned ruins and place name evidence reveal a once vibrant, populous community with a rich Gaelic culture, working and living with nature, albeit in extreme weathers.

The track crosses Allt Loch an t-Sidhein and to the left a small path heads up to a fenced field. To the left of the path, a burnt heather clad hillock is the shian or fairy hill, which though no longer marked on maps, is recorded in the place names of the immediate area: Allt Loch an t-Sidhein, Rygean, Loch an t-Sidhein and Blaar Loch an t-Sidhean. At the southern end of the field a fallen tree and a few stones are all that's left of Rygean (shieling of the fairy hill). The track goes on to Loch an t-Sidhein or return to the main track on the right, which gradually climbs towards the pass between Cam Sgriob and Carn Slioch. This is an old route from Lochindorb to the Dulnain and Spey and may have been that taken by Edward I and his army in 1303. Returning by the same route, small detours can be made to explore the ruins of Cairnloch and the former township of Glentarroch.

2: Lochindorb to Shendale

Beyond the entrance to Lochindorb Lodge, on the left and almost where the plantation stops, a track leads through to Corrycharcle (hoop shaped corrie). Formerly abandoned, it has now been restored as a lunch hut for estate guests, out shooting on the 'Glorious Twelfth'. Like many of the abandoned farms on the moor, it was probably a shieling and appears on Pont's 16th century map. Later it's recorded as an improvement and was long held by the Frasers, an old Dava family, who also had connections to Easter and Wester Limekilns. It's a bit surreal standing here among the last remnants of an ancient forest, surrounded by a variety of trees covered in lichens and mosses. Hard to believe such an oasis exists on the Dava. As the road climbs Carn nan Gabhar (hill of the goats), take time to look back over to Lochindorb and its castle. The 13th century fortalice was built by the Comyn family, opponents to Bruce in the Wars of Independence. Its most famous resident was Alexander Stewart, the Wolf of Badenoch whose notoriety arose for burning Elgin Cathedral, following his excommunication. It later passed into the hands of the Douglas family and was ordered to be demolished following their fall from grace in 1455.

Descend the other side to the House of Glengour. Once a substantial residence, only the back wall and gables remain. Behind it, hidden in the gorse bushes, is the older Glengour settlement. The encroaching gorse has almost engulfed the remaining buildings and well preserved corn drying kiln.

Returning back down the hill to the track, follow it right and patches of green fields are visible in the distance. Clues that further settlements were once here. The first is Ryluachrach (shieling of the rushes) and a little further on Shendale (old meadow). Camerons once lived here until the late 19th century. Probably giving up the struggle, once the railway to Inverness and Perth opened a station at Dava in 1863.

3: Routes from the Jesus Saves Stone

The final walk on the western side of the A939 starts at 'The Jesus Saves' stone. A well-known landmark to drivers in the area, its origins are somewhat now an urban myth. Several explanations have been put forward, but the one recounted to me by a native Dava resident, recounts a motorcyclist came off his bike and was saved by the stone from certain death. In gratitude he painted it with the familiar inscription. The road was realigned and originally the boulder was on the other side. Whatever the origin of the story, there's at least one anonymous individual who religiously maintains the boulder and ensures a fresh coat of paint is applied as required.

Perhaps the fairies, residing in the fairy hill (Sidhean an Aiteil), close to the Jesus Saves Stone were also as benevolent to passers-bye in an earlier age. The track from here joins the Old Military Road passed Loch Mhic Leoid to Anaboard. The stretch beyond Anaboard to Camerory still has hollows on either side, where stones were quarried for its construction in 1755. It's not hard to imagine Redcoats patrolling this area between Fort George and Corgarff or the cattle drovers that passed this way south to the trysts at Falkirk and Crieff.

From Loch Mhic Leoid the track west leads past Loch na Cloiche Muilinn (loch of the mill stone) probably due to its round shape, and up to Easter and Wester Crannich (place of trees). Once home to MacDonalds, well known fiddle players here about, the farm steading retains some interesting features. There's a circular structure retained by a low dyke, that was once the area where the horses walked round, powering the corn thrasher in the barn. Within the roofless barn the walls still retain large rotting tree trunks or couples, which once supported the thatched roof. Until the early 20th century, many properties in the area were still roofed with divots and heather thatch. The houses gradually became slated once cheaper slates from Wales could be obtained, imported by the railways. The out buildings had to make do with corrugated iron sheets, which now make colourful rust red blotches in the landscape.

The next property is Rychorrach (steep shieling or sheep shieling) which was still semi occupied by the Smith family of Dreggie until the early 1970's. Perched on the side of Carn Ruigh Chorrach (484 m,1587 ft), it looks south over the moor towards the Cairgorms, a great view when the hills are capped with snow. The track eventually joins up at Glengour where it can be linked to walks 1 or 2, or return to the Jesus Saves Stone.

4: Dava to Sgor Gaoithe and Ourack

The eastern side of the Dava moor was less populated and suited to agriculture. From the A939 at Dava, a hill track from the Dava

Way heads up hill towards Aittendow (place of black juniper). The former farm house is built near the old shieling of Rue Uan (shieling of the lamb) and the ruins of the original Aittendow are further east. There is some confusion on the Ordinance Survey maps for this area. Names of settlements and hills have been allocated to different features, according to the original 18th and 19th century estate maps. South of Aittendow a lone larch tree marks the site of Rychraggan (shieling of the rocks) long inhabited by the Paterson family.

Tracks can be followed making for the summit of Carn na Glaisneach (hill of the horse hollow) and beyond to Carn Bad na Caorach (hill of the sheep clump 477m. 1564 ft)

From the cairn head north east to the fence that bisects the hill road from Auchnagallin to Ourack. Follow the fence from the gate to the rocky outcrop of Sgor Gaoithe (rock of the wind). On the watershed between Strathspey and the Dava Moor, it has one of the finest panoramic views. It exposes to all the senses, what the Dava conveys to so many that have lived or walked it.

Follow the hill road that was probably the Via Regia, due north past the solitary chimney stack of Badahad, a former gamekeepers isolated residence and by the burn crossing a ford, beside the remains of the shieling of Allt Tarsin. The road turns left up the hill back to Aittendow, but a little beyond the bend on the opposite bank the ruins of the Ourack are worth a visit.

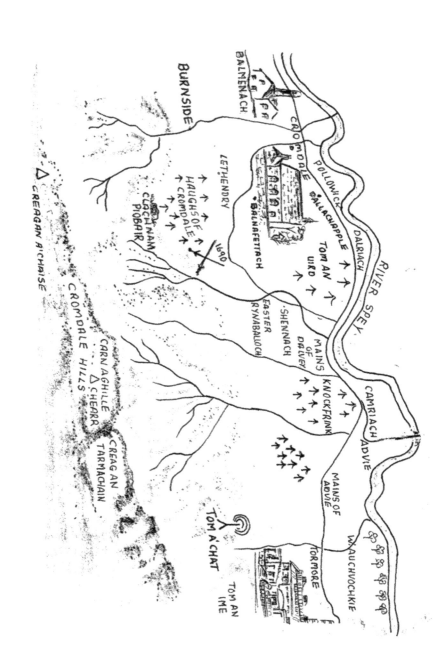

BALMENACH

BURNSIDE

CREAGAN A'CHAISE

CROMDALE

POLLOWICK

DALLACHAPPLE

DALRIACH

RIVER SPEY

LETHENDRY

HAUGHS OF CROMDALE

CLACH NAM PIOBAIR

BALNAFETTACH

1690

TOM AN UIRD

EASTER RYNABALLOCH

SHENNACH

MAINS OF DALVEY

KNOCKFRINK

CAMRIACH

ADVIE

CROMDALE HILLS

CARN AGHILLE

SHEARR

CREAG AN TARMACHAIN

MAINS OF ADVIE

TOM A'CHAT

TORMORE

WAUCHVOCHKIE

TOM AN IME

CHAPTER 7

Cromdale

Davochs 1767

Barony of Cromdale

Claigernach, Ballichule, Easter Lethendy, Wester Lethendy (Mains of Lethendy), Cottartown of Lethendy, Croft of Lethendy, Culnduim, Croftindam, Achrosk, Croftnastree, Burnside of Bellameanach, Lyne of Burnside, Corn milne & Milntown of Cromdale, Tomlia, Upper Belmeanoch, Nether Belmeanoch, Torran na biach, Bruntland, Croft Malloch, Knock of Achroisk, Achroisk, Westertown of Achroisk, Town of Cromdale, improvements of Rysmutan.

Davoch of Rynabeallich

Easter Rynabeallich, Wester Rynabeallich, Mains of Dellachaple, Waulkmiln, Pollawick, Tominourd, Balnafettack, Tomnanceann, Starindoai, Balnabottach, improvements of Upper Rynabeallich, Alinnanghatt, Drimnacoinach

Davoch of Dalvey

Shenval and Upper & Nether Alteuans, Aird, Easter Shennach, Wester Shennach, Belnailen, Achnearnach, Knocknaeulich, Milntown of Dalvey, Delriach, Mains of Dalvey, Easter Delriach, Cairnglass, Duiar,

Davoch of Wester Skiradvie

Advie, Knocknean, Knockfrenk, Mains of Advie, Mains of Dellay, Miln & Miln Croft of Dellay, Newton of Dellay, Deldow of Newton, Deldow, Camriach, Diuar improvement, Corresheallach improvement, Improvement above Cameriach, Improvement above Newtown.

Davoch of Easter Skiradvie

Easter Achvochkie, Toremore, Glebe of Skiradvy, Airdbeg, Rinrory, Wester & Mid Achvouchkies, Garvalt, Corresheallach improvement, Fanemore improvement

Achnanerich: 1841   Auchnearanach 1767

Achvochkie Burn: NJ 1488 3526

A small burn at the east side of Easter Achvochkie. It enters the Spey opposite Dalchroy. [OSNB]

Achvochkie Cottage: NJ 1480 3476

A thatched dwelling house having outhouses attached. [OSNB]

Easter Achvochkie: NJ 1477 3533   1841, 1851

A thatched dwelling house having outhouses attached. [OSNB]

Fields: The Folds, Fyarlachan. 1804

Mid Achvockie: 1804

Wester Achvochkie: 1851   NJ 146 350

A slated farm house having outhouses attached. [OSNB]

Advie: Place of birch   NJ 1279 3461   Skiradvie

Parish or 'shire' of Advie

Advie Old Parish Cemetery: NJ 1418 3528

Advie Station: NJ 1274 3459

A former third class station built of wood with waiting area attached on the Strathspey section, situated between Ballindalloch Station and Cromdale. [OSNB]

Mill of Advie: 1851   NJ 1378 3418

A meal mill of one storey worked by water, thatched and in good repair. [OSNB]

Advie School: NJ 1239 3429

A handsome stone building with dwelling house for master attached. It is a parish school maintained by the heritors. The scholars are of both sexes and the average attendance is about 35 daily. [OSNB]

Glebe of Skiradvy: by old church 1804

Mains of Advie: NJ 1372 3427   1804, 1851

A slated farm house, two storeys high, having extensive outhouses attached. [OSNB]

Airdbeg: Little high place   NJ 1420 3404   Ardbeg 1804, 1841, Airdbegg 1851

A small farm steading, situated a little south of Advie Post Office. [OSNB]

Field: Bog Buie. 1804

Aird of Dalvey: 1851   High place   NJ 1139 3122

A small farm steading and dwelling house of one storey in good repair with garden attached. [OSNB]

Fields: The Meikle Fae, Calves Park, Craig Du, Bualich Fold, Sual Glass, The Chapple

Allanmore: 1841 The big meadow   NJ 1002 2922, NJ 1001 2856

Two farm houses, each of which are one storey high, thatched and in good repair. [OSNB]

Allt a'Cheannaiche: The merchant's burn   NJ 1087 2781

A small burn having its source at the western base of the Hills of Cromdale and flowing in a north westerly direction past the farm steading of Corsheallach. [OSNB]

Allt a'Chreagain: Burn of the little rocks   NJ 1339 3112

A small burn rising a little north west of Carn Gillie Chere and after a northerly course of about one mile it is called the Burn of Advie. [OSNB]

Allt an Torra Mhoir: Burn of the large hillock   NJ 1552 3484

A small burn rising at the north of Carn Mor and joining the Burn of Achvochkie at the Bridge of Tormore. [OSNB]

Allt Creag an Tarmachain: Burn of the rock of the ptarmigan   NJ 1391 3112

This burn rises on the south west side of Creagan Ptarmigan and flows north west ward. It receives the waters of the Middle Strype and is then joined by Allt Creagan. The three waters forming the Burn of Advie. [OSNB]

Allt Eoghainn: Ewan's Burn   NJ 1234 3069

A small burn rising a little north of Tom na Sealgair and after a northerly course of about two miles flows into the River Spey about half a mile east of the Mains of Dalvey. [OSNB]

Allt Eoghainn Bhig: Little burn of Euan   NJ 1144 2898

A small burn having its source at the north western base of the Hills of Cromdale and flowing in a westerly direction until it joins Allt na Criche near to Easter Rynabeallich. [OSNB]

Allt MhicNeacail: Nicolson or McNicol's Burn   NJ 1055 2732

A small burn having its source at the north western base of the Hills of Cromdale and flowing in a westerly direction past Craggan farm steading. [OSNB]

Allt na Criche: Burn of the boundary   NJ 1221 2914

A burn having its source at the north western base of the Hills of Cromdale and flowing in a westerly direction until it joins Dalvey Burn a little north of Eastern Rynaballoch. It was formerly the boundary between the Counties of Inverness and Moray. [OSNB]

Allt na Croite: Burn of the croft   NJ 1168 2814

A burn having its source at the western base of the Hills of Cromdale and flowing in a north westerly direction until it joins Allt Eoghainn Bhig, close to the farm house of Easter Rynabeallich. [OSNB]

Allt na h'Airidhe: Burn of the shieling   NJ 0960 2644

A burn having its source at the western base of the Hills of Cromdale and flowing in a westerly direction. [OSNB]

An Deanntag: The nettle   NJ 1495 3550

A heathy hill feature north east of Wester Auchvochkie. [OSNB]

An Leacann: NJ 1448 3316

Applied to a steep hill feature of considerable height, situated about half a mile west of Carn Mor. [OSNB]

Auldyoun: Burn of the bird or Ewen's Burn   NJ 1181 3123
Aldioun 1841, Aldyoun 1851

A small farm steading and dwelling house of one storey, thatched and in good repair. [OSNB]

Auchroisk: Field of the crossing or cross roads   NJ 0725 2848
Achroisk 1851

A farm steading, dwelling house and offices, one storey high, slated and in good repair. [OSNB]

Westertown of Achroisk: 1851

Ballachule: Homestead of the nook or back   NJ 0903 2751
Balchule 1851

A farm steading consisting of a dwelling house and three out houses all one storey high and in middling condition. [OSNB]

Ballindian: Clump of the hill face   NJ 0879 2839

A farmhouse and out offices, one storey high, thatched and in good repair. [OSNB]

Balmenach: The middle homestead   Bellymenoch 1767, 1841, 1851

Fields: Achindoul, Shaint

Balmenach Distillery: NJ 0781 2717

This name is applied to a two storey dwelling house, office houses and a number of houses in which the distillation of whisky is carried on. The whole of these, except the dwelling house are one storey high and all are in very good condition. It is the property and residence of Mr McGregor. [OSNB]

Lower Balmenach: NJ 0771 2783 1841 Nether Balmenach

A farm steading consisting of a dwelling house and an outhouse, both are thatched and in good condition. [OSNB]

Field: Dau Cruie

Balnaboddach: Homestead of the old man   NJ 0772 2835 Balnabottach 1841

A farmhouse and out offices, one storey high, thatched, in good repair. [OSNB]

Fields: Dallu Fleugh, The Drum. 1809

Balnafettock: Homestead of the plover NJ 0869 2891 Bellnafettack 1767, Balnafetack 1841, 1851

A farmhouse and out offices, one storey high, thatched and in good repair. [OSNB]

Fields: Bual More, Losit, Knockan Tailor, Touminourd, Tor Crochie, Dallu Fleugh, Creachdu. 1809

Balnallan: Homestead of the plain or meadow   Balnalan 1841

Applied to a good substantial farm steading of one story thatched and in good repair with garden and dwelling house attached. [OSNB]

Fields: Meikle Fold, The Broom Hillock

Balvlair: NJ 1062 3055

This name applies to two dwelling houses built of stone, thatched and in good repair with gardens and a few acres of land attached. [OSNB]

Battle of Cromdale: NJ 1030 2775   Haughs of Cromdale [OSNB]

30 April/ 1 May 1690 where the Jacobite force under General Buchan was surprised and defeated by government army commanded by Sir Thomas Livingstone.

Biggie's Howe: NJ 1557 3535

A small hollow east of Tormore Farm.

Black Burn: NJ 1046 3088

A small burn which rises at the eastern extremity of the hill Tom an Uird and after a north easterly course of about quarter of a mile becomes confluent with the Burn of Dalvey near the farm of Balnallan. [OSNB]

Blackward: NJ 1458 3455   Black Waird 1812

Thatched dwelling house having blacksmith's shop attached. [OSNB]

Bog: NJ 1291 3502   Bogg 1851

Applied to a good substantial farm steading of one storey built with stone, thatched and in good repair. [OSNB]

Bog Buie: Yellow bog or quagmire   NJ 1483 3444

A small moss north east of Blackward. [OSNB]

Bridge of Advie: NJ 1373 3376   Burn of Skiradvy 1804

A bridge of one arch spanning the Burn of Advie. [OSNB]

Bridge of Dalvey: NJ 1092 3216

A neat substantial stone bridge which crosses the Burn of Dalvey, situated on the road leading from Advie to Grantown. [OSNB]

Bridge of Duier: NJ 1200 3314

A small stone bridge on the turnpike road crossing the Burn of Duier a short distance from where it joins the Spey. [OSNB]

Bridge of Shennach: NJ 1114 2983

A neat wooden bridge which crosses the Burn of Dalvey a little south of the farm Easter Shennach. [OSNB]

Bridge of Tormore: NJ 1536 3503

A bridge of one arch spanning the Burn of Tormore on the road leading to Grantown. [OSNB]

Bruntland: Burnt or scorched land   NJ 0733 2760   Bruntlands 1841, Bruntland 1851

Two cottages under one roof, one storey high, thatched and in bad condition. [OSNB]

The Bruntland Scape (island) 1804

Burn of Advie: NJ 1373 3376 [OSNB]

Burn of Coire Seileach: NJ 1386 3259

A small burn commencing its name from Allt Creagan and retaining it to the Burn of Garvault. [OSNB]

Burn of Cromdale: NJ 0752 2830

A burn that flows past the farm steading of Tomlea and into the River Spey near the parish church of Cromdale. Between Tomlea and its junction with the River Spey it is called Burn of Cromdale and above Tomlea it is called Allt Chuine. [OSNB]

Burn of Dalvey: NJ 1078 3171

A small burn rising near the centre of the Cromdale Hills, which following a northerly direction for about two and a half miles, becomes confluent with the River Spey near the Mains of Dalvey. [OSNB]

Burn of Duier: NJ 1214 3288

A small burn rising a little south of the moors of Knockfrink and flowing north until it flows into the River Spey near Bridge of Duier. [OSNB]

Burn of Garvault: NJ 1457 3265

A small mountain stream rising about half a mile south of Carn Mor called in the upper part of its course, Redwell Burn and after a westerly course of about a mile and a half flows into the Burn of Advie. [OSNB]

Burnside: NJ 08170 2614   1841, 1851

A large farm steading consisting of two dwelling houses and extensive office houses. One of the dwelling houses is two storeys high, the rest of the buildings are one storey high and in very good condition. [OSNB]

Fields: Garland, Lagleuch, Balnlae, Ecachan, Tornmolt, Toumnamoin, Cnochendoul, Achsalter

Cairns: NJ 1206 3261

A number of small irregular conical piles of stones, said to have been erected over the slain in a conflict while opposing the invasion of the Danes. [OSNB]

Callinduim: Back of the little hill   NJ 0861 2648   Culinduin 1841, 1851

An untenanted farm steading consisting of a dwelling house offices and a small thrashing mill. The whole of them in a very poor condition. [OSNB]

Cambrae: The crooked brae   NJ 0742 2830   Cambreach

Cameriach: The brindle bend or curve   NJ 1177 3402   Camriach 1804

Applied to a crofters dwelling house built chiefly of wood one storey, in good repair with a few acres attached. [OSNB]

Cnoc nan Eun: The birds hill   NJ 1339 3438

A small hill west of the Mains of Advie. [OSNB]

Caochannaneun: Hill of the birds   NJ 1346 3442   Knockanain 1841, 1851

A thatched dwelling house having outhouses attached. [OSNB]

Caochan Fiarach: The twisting burn   NJ 1433 3469

A small burn rising at Bog Buie and forming Caochan Luadh, west of Blackward. [OSNB]

Caochan Ruadh: Red burn   NJ 1419 3439

A small burn rising at the north west side of Carn Mor and joining the Burn of Advie, south west of the old church of Advie. [OSNB]

Carn a' Ghille Chear: Hill of the left handed boy   NJ 1396 2985 Carn Machk Gillie Chere 1804,

One of the most prominent of the Cromdale Hills, situated about a mile and a half south of Knock Frink. [OSNB]

Carn a' Mhaoisleich: Hill of the roe deer   NJ 1542 3580

A small hill situated at the eastern extremity of the parish, rumour says that women perished here during a storm by the name of Mhaoisidh, hence the name. [OSNB]

Carn Mor: Large ridge   NJ 1565 3319

A prominent hill situated near the east of the parish. [OSNB]

Carn na h-Iolaire   Hill of the eagle   NJ 1253 2955   Tom na h-Iolaire

A prominent hill situated about a mile and a half south of the farm Auldyoun. [OSNB]

Castle Lethendry: Lethendry Castle   NJ 0841 2740

The ruins of an old 16th century castle at the farm steading of Wester Lethendry. The ruins consist of one large vault encompassed on the east and south by a large high wall which was formerly the principal wall of the castle. [OSNB] Formerly the property of the Nairn family, it was sold to the Laird of Grant.

Clach nan Coileach: The Cocks Stone   NJ 1446 3567

A large stone north of Achvochkie Burn and east side of the River Spey. [OSNB]

Clach nam Piobair: Stone of the pipers   NJ 1030 2693

A large stone about 5ft high by 3 or 4ft in circumference. Situated at the eastern extremity of the Haughs of Cromdale. [OSNB] It is said to be the stone where the pipers of the Jacobite army played during the battle.

Claggersnich: Noise of horses   NJ 0910 2808   Clagersnich 1851

A farmhouse and out offices from one to two storeys high, partly thatched and partly slated, in good repair. [OSNB]

Field: Crochk Gyllum

Cnoc na Seilg: Knoll of the hunt   NJ 1175 2898

A prominent hill situated at the north west shoulder of the Cromdale Hills. [OSNB]

Cordon Burn: The deep hollow   NJ 0929 2492

A small burn rising at the north east base of the Cromdale Hills, flowing in a north westerly direction until it joins Riesnuttan Burn. [OSNB]

Corshellach: Willow hollow   NJ 1049 2796 Corryshellach 1809, 1841,

A farm house and out offices one storey high, thatched and in good repair. [OSNB]

Fields: Dreim a Choinich 1809

Cottertown: The cotter's town   NJ 0802 2764   1841,

Two very small cottages and one out house all one storey high and in middling condition. [OSNB]

Fields: Knockean Baan, Baul McRobert

Craggan: NJ 0999 2781

A farm house and out offices one storey high, thatched and in middling repair. [OSNB]

Crait: 1809 Croft

Craitnamollacht: Croft of the rough places   NJ 0741 2801 Croftnmolach 1841, Croftnamolachd 1851

A farm steading consisting of a dwelling house and an outhouse, both thatched and in middling condition. [OSNB]

Creag an Tarmachain: NJ 1521 3098 Craggan Tormagan 1804

A high hill in the south eastern corner of the former parish, on whose rocky crag named after the Ptarmigan. [OSNB]

Creagan Mor: Big rocky place NJ 1444 3582

A large rock on the south side of the River Spey and about a mile west of the farm Fanmore. [OSNB]

Creag nan Cat: Rock of the cats NJ 1314 3041

A solitary rock situated on a prominent position on the Cromdale Hills. [OSNB]

Croftindam: Croft of the mill dam   NJ 0796 2799   1841, 1851

A farm steading consisting of two houses, one dwelling house both thatched and in middling condition. [OSNB]

Cromdale: Curved dale   NJ 075 285 [OSNB]

Auchroisk Place: NJ 0729 2841

Balmeanach Road: NJ 0741 2833

Cambrae: NJ 0741 2835

Cromdale Bridge: 1841   NJ 074 284   Bridge End of Cromdale
1851

Cromdale Church: NJ 0666 2896

Built in 1809 and much altered about 1895. Built on site of older church.

Cromdale Inn: NJ 0767 2882 New Inn of Cromdale 1851

A public house and farm steading, partly thatched and partly slated, from one to two storeys high, in good repair. [OSNB]

Cromdale Manse: NJ 0681 2890   1841, 1851

A commodious house situated about 6 chains east of the church. It is from two to 3 storeys high, slated in good repair. The property of the Heritors of the parish of Cromdale, Inverallan and Advie. [OSNB]

Cromdale Post Office: NJ 0752 2856

A commodious house part of which is used as a grocers shop. It is one storey high, slated, in good repair. The arrivals and departures at this office are as follows. Arrive 8:30 am depart 2:30 pm. [OSNB]

Cromdale School: NJ 0676 2850

The parish school where the elementary branches of education are taught by a master. There is an average attendance of about 60 scholars. It is one storey high, slated and in good repair. [OSNB]

Cromdale Station: NJ 0711 2864

A station on the Great North of Scotland Railway. One storey high, slated in good repair. The property of the Great North of Scotland Railway Company. [OSNB]

Kirk Road: NJ 0711 2847

Sandys Way: NJ 0727 2826

The Haugh: NJ 0753 2855

The Old Station: NJ 0708 2854

Dail na Rainich: Dale of the bracken   NJ 1452 3610

A piece of arable land situated a little south east of Balnacraobh. [OSNB]

Dalchapple: Field of the mare (horse) NJ 0813 2934 Dellichapple 1841, Dallachapele 1851

A farm house and out offices from one to two storeys high, thatched and in good repair. [OSNB]

Fields: Coinach, Dreim Voulin, Lag hough, Creach Du, Laggan Chapple. 1809

Dalchapple Burn: NJ 0830 2919

A burn arising at the junction of Allt a' Cheannaiche and Allt Mhc Neacail and flowing in a westerly direction until it enters the River Spey, west of Dalchapple farmsteading.[OSNB]

Dale of Advie: NJ 1308 3489

An extensive piece of flat land which extends from near the farm of Camriach to about half a mile east of the farm Bog, a distance of two miles. [OSNB]

Dalvey: NJ 1102 3215   Mains of Dalvey

A large superior farm steading of one storey, slated and in good repair, with dwelling house attached. [OSNB]

Fields: Burnside Park, Poind, Old Park, Fidlers Park, Meikle Cairn Park, Kinglass Park, Drynach, The Meikle Park, Broad Folds, The Claddach

Dalvey Farm Halt:

A small railway station halt on the Speyside route. It opened on 15 June 1959 and closed 18 Oct 1965.

Delay: Birch field   NJ 1381 3495   1841

A farm house now in ruins, having outhouses etc attached. All in a state of ruins. [OSNB]

Field: Haugh of Delay. 1804

Deldow: Dark field   NJ 1242 3508   1841

A small farmsteading of one storey situated about half a mile north of Advie Station. [OSNB]

Fields: The Bogg, Ellan na Muchk (island). 1804

Easter Delriach: Brindled field   NJ 0873 3158   1841,

A crofter's dwelling house with offices and garden attached of one storey and in good repair. [OSNB]

Wester Delriach:

A farm steading & dwellinghouse, one storey high, thatched & in good repair. [OSNB]

Duier: Grove or thicket   NJ 1199 3340   The Duir 1804, 1841

A croft dwelling houses of one storey, built with stone, thatched and in good repair. [OSNB]

Eilean na Cloiche: Island of the stone   NJ 1395 3532

A portion of ground west of Advie Old Church. It is covered with whins, rough pasture, shingle and brush wood. The channel of the river having altered it is now attached to the shore. [OSNB]

Eilean na Muic: Island of the pig   NJ 1255 3540 Eilean na Muchk 1804

A small island partly cultivated, situated a little north of the farm of Deldow. [OSNB]

Fanmore: Large area of low ground   NJ 1546 3638 Faan More 1804, 1841

A good substantial farm steading in good repair situated near the east of the parish. [OSNB]

Field: Shihan More. 1804

Feabuie: Yellow bog   NJ 0678 2700   1841, 1851

Five croft houses, they are all one storey high, thatched and in indifferent condition. [OSNB]

Fuaranbuie: The Yellow spring   NJ 1024 2781   1841

A farm house and out offices one storey high thatched and in middling repair. [OSNB]

Garbh-ath Mor: The Large Ford   NJ 0767 2941

A ford on the River Spey, situated north west of the farmsteading of Starindeye. Tradition points to this as being the spot where government troops forded the Spey on their march to the battle of the Haughs of Cromdale. [OSNB]

Garden Cottage: NJ 1596 3560

A thatched cottage with outhouses and gardens attached at the eastern extremity of the parish. [OSNB]

Garvault: Rough or stony burn   NJ 1384 3369   Garvalt 1841,

A good substantial farm steading and dwelling house of one storey, thatched and in good repair with out houses and garden attached. Situated about half a mile south of Advie Post Office. [OSNB]

Field: Led Ochku more. 1804

Haughs of Cromdale: Low lying land beside the Spey   NJ 0946 2742

30 April/ 1 May 1690 where the Jacobite force under General Buchan was surprised and defeated by government army commanded by Sir Thomas Livingstone. [OSNB]

Hills of Cromdale: Cromdale Hills   NJ 1157 2686

A chain of hills extending over a distance of 7 or 8 miles in a north and south direction and forming the southern boundary of the former parish. [OSNB]

Hill of Lethendry: Hill of the Laird's half   NJ 0876 2690   Tom of Lethendry

A small hill situated about half a mile south east of Wester Lethendry. [OSNB]

Inverguichan: NJ 0936 2844   1841

A croft house with suitable offices, one storey high, thatched, in good repair. [OSNB]

Kirkton of Cromdale: NJ 0669 2849

Site of planned village near church.

Knockfrink: NJ 1363 3343   1851

A small dwelling house in good repair, situated a little east of the Hill of Knock Frink. [OSNB]

Fields: Garbol, Knockan na Muirich. 1804

Knock Frink: NJ 1309 3293   1841

Woods of Knockfrink: NJ 1264 3300

A wood of considerable extent, situated a little south of Advie Station. [OSNB]

Knocknahyl: Hillock of limestone   NJ 0851 2833   Torannahail 1851,

A farmhouse and out offices one storey high, thatched and in good repair. [OSNB]

Laggandhu: The little black hollow   NJ 1108 2883

A farm house and out offices one storey high, thatched and in good repair. [OSNB]

Easter Lethendry: NJ 0854 2774   The laird's half   1767, 1851

A large farm steading consisting of a two storey dwelling house and seven office houses, the former slated and in middling condition and the latter are one storey high, thatched and in indifferent condition. [OSNB]

Fields: The Cruchkan, Crait Mariat, Crochk Yetsich, Meikle Balnastock

Wester Lethendry: NJ 0841 2745   1767, 1851

A farm steading consisting of a dwelling house and out houses all one storey high and in good condition. [OSNB]

Lochinoir: Loch of gold   NJ 1589 3587   Lochineoir 1851

A small dwelling house of one storey in good repair with a few acres of land and gardens attached. [OSNB]

Mains of Cromdale: NJ 0682 2851   1851

A farmhouse and out offices one storey high, partly thatched and partly slated in good repair. [OSNB]

Meiklepark Wood: Big park   NJ 1139 3167

A birch wood which extends from near the farm of Balnallan to the burn of Allt Eoghainn. [OSNB]

Middle Strype: Middle burn or ditch   NJ 1361 3117

A burn which flows into the Allt Creagan Tarmachain. [OSNB]

Mill of Dalvey: NJ 1085 3176

A meal mill of one storey worked by water in good repair. [OSNB]

Milton: NJ 1058 3211

A small farm steading of one storey with dwelling house attached. [OSNB]

Milton of Cromdale: NJ 0765 2815

A corn mill, farm house and out offices, one storey high, thatched, in good repair. [OSNB]

Moss Burn: NJ 1435 3186

A small burn in the south eastern part of the parish. It flows into the Burn of Garvault after a run of a mile. [OSNB]

Newtown:

Fields: The Haugh, Meikle Isle, Feacharabit. 1804

Pollowick: 1767   Pool of the pig

Fields: Haugh of Pollowick, Dell Cruy, Knock Brack, Del More. 1809

Pollowick Easter: NJ 0812 3010   1851

A farm steading & dwelling house, one story high thatched & in good repair. [OSNB]

Pollowick Wester: NJ 0808 3000   1851

A farm steading & dwelling House, one story high, thatched & in good repair. [OSNB]

Red Well: NJ 1559 3257

A chalybeate spring of water impregnated with iron situated about half a mile south of Carn Mor. [OSNB]

Redwell Burn: NJ 1577 3250

Part of a burn rising about a mile south of Carn Mor and after a westerly course of little more than a quarter of a mile it is called the Back Burn. [OSNB]

Riesnuttan Burn: Shieling of the wood pigeon   NJ 0956 2556
Resmudan Burn

A small burn rising at the western base of the Cromdale Hills and flowing in a westerly direction. [OSNB]

Easter Rynabeallich: The shieling of the pass   NJ 1098 2937
Rynaballich 1841, Easter Rynaballich 1851

A farm house and out offices one storey high, thatched and in good repair. [OSNB]

Fields: Ouchka Baan, Ballavattan, Lack Bellavattan, Loin, Crochtich, Delllagan du. 1809

Mid Rynaballich: 1851

Fields: Laggan Du 1809

Wester Rynabeallich: NJ 1066 2881   1851

A farm house and out offices, one storey high, thatched and in good repair. [OSNB]

Fields: Prae Beg, Guilach Cuil, Losit, Keaunach More. 1809

Rynrory: 1851   Reddish coloured shieling

Shanvell: Old farmstead   NJ 1202 3200   Shenval 1841

A small thatched dwelling house of one storey, used as a cottar house on the farm of Mains of Dalvey. [OSNB]

Shennach (Easter)   Old field   Easter Shenach 1841

Applied to a good substantial farm steading and dwelling house of one story in good repair with a small garden attached. [OSNB]

Field: Bruchk n Leish

Shennach (Wester)   Wester Shenach 1841

Applied to a small farm steading and dwelling house of one story with out houses and gardens attached the property. [OSNB]

Starindeye: The rough point with a house on it   NJ 0777 2917   Starrindoaie 1767, Sterindeigh 1841, Stirindeigh 1851, Sturendey

A farmhouse and out houses, one storey high, thatched and in good repair. [OSNB]

Fields: Craitn Rosick, Dallu Fleugh, Knockan Ruag, Dreim Voulin. 1809

Sithean Beag: Little fairy hillock   NJ 1505 3605

A small fairy hill a little south west of Fanmore. [OSNB]

Sithean Mor: Big fairy hillock   NJ 1514 3618

A fairy hillock a little west of the farm of Fanmore. [OSNB]

Sithean na Faile Moire: NJ 1503 3568

A small hill east of Easter Achvochie and north of Tormore farm houses. [OSNB]

Strype of Logieyouse: Stream or ditch of the pine hollow   NJ 1540 3231   Lagaguish

A small burn in the south east part of the parish, flowing into the Redwell Burn after a course of about half a mile. [OSNB]

Tom a' Chat   Hillock of the cat

Tom an Ime: The butter hillock   NJ 1610 3479

A small hill planted a little south of Garden Cottage. [OSNB]

Tom an Uird: Hill of the hammer   Tomenourd 1767, Tominourd 1809 [OSNB]

Field: Tor Crochie 1809

Tomlea: Grey knoll   NJ 0767 2621   Tomliah 1841

A small farm steading consisting of a dwelling house and two offices, all thatched and in middling condition. [OSNB]

Upper Tomlea: NJ 0764 2541

A small steading, dwelling house and offices, thatched, one storey high and in good repair. [OSNB]

Tom Liath: Grey knoll   NJ 0707 2595

A hill situated at the south end of the parish, over the top of which passed the boundary between the parishes of Cromdale, Inverallan and Advie and Abernethy and Kincardine. [OSNB]

Tom na Coinnich: Foggy hillock or moss hillock   NJ 1390 3152

A small hill forming as it were a step to the west side of Ptarmigan's Crag. [OSNB]

Tom nan Culagan: Hillock of peat turf   NJ 1527 3457

A hill feature east of Achvochkie farm. A hill where sods used to be cut for the purpose of putting behind the fire. [OSNB]

Tomnagaun: Stirk's hillock   NJ 0846 2898   1841, Tomnageann 1809

A farmhouse and out offices, one storey high, thatched, in good repair. [OSNB]

Fields: Knock Cruy, Dallu Luisk, Laggan Chapple, Creach More, Knockan a Ha, Allan a Gat. 1809

Torinruich: Red hillock   NJ 1026 2821   Toranrich 1851

A farm house and out offices one storey high, thatched and in good repair. [OSNB]

Field: Allan More 1809

Tormore: Big hill   NJ 1533 3516   1841

A slated farm house having outhouses etc attached, all in good repair. [OSNB]

Field: Baul Bain. 1804

Torran Glas: Grey hillock   NJ 1513 3520

A small hillock west of Tormore. [OSNB]

Tuessis: NJ 0674 2840

Appears on the 1st edition 6" Ordnance Survey maps as a Roman encampment beside the Spey. Ptolemy wrote in the second century A.D. of such a place in northern Scotland, and from the description early 19th century antiquarians attributed it to this spot. There is no written or archaeological evidence to support the claims. [OSNB]

Waukmill: NJ 0753 2889

A farmhouse and out offices one storey high, thatched and in good repair. [OSNB]

Fields: Fual a Vaan, Dallu Fleugh. 1809

Walks

Starting at the lay-by opposite Cromdale kirk, cross the fence and walk along the river bank towards the road bridge. A sandy patch on the grass bank, which used to be more obvious, marks the site of St Ma Luaig's well. An Irish saint and contemporary of Columba, he helped spread Christianity amongst the Picts in the 6th century. He established religious centres at Mortlach near Dufftown and Rosemarkie on the Black Isle. The spot gives a good view of Cromdale Church, which has served the parish for centuries despite the problem of access for many parishioners. 'It was by no means convenient to the great bulk of the population', for until a wire suspension bridge was built in 1881, the only way was by ferry. The Boat of Cromdale, where the ferryman lived is a short distance downstream on the left.

The first bridge did not last long, being washed away in 1894. A second bridge had a similar fate in 1921, so a more substantial bridge of girders from World War I surplus was erected in 1922. The piers of the earlier bridge can still be seen.

The church is of simple plain construction dating from 1809, built on a much earlier site. There are many interesting gravestones with a preponderance of Grants!

Continue along the road past the impressive former manse and on approaching the bridge over the former railway line, look left at the restored Cromdale Station. Now a private residence, it sits on a stretch of the Strathspey Way. Turn left at the crossroads (Achroisk, field of crossing) and over another bridge that crosses the Burn of Cromdale. At the junction beside the former school built in 1877, turn right and walk up the straight road past Balnaboddach (farmstead of the old man) and Croftindam.

As the road bends to the left, take the side road on the right to Easter and Wester Lethendry. Information boards give historical background about the Battle of the Haughs of Cromdale and way markers point the direction to the Pipers Stone and Lethendry Castle.

A circular walk from here can be taken to Wester Lethendry and the castle. Beyond the farm steading, the ruins of the 16th century castle rise above later farm buildings that have been built into its walls. The castle once belonged to the Nairn family and formed part of the Barony of Cromdale. The lands were later purchased by the Lairds of Grant. After the Battle of the Haughs of Cromdale, some Jacobites held out here, but were eventually captured. Return to Easter Lethendry and turn right past the farm house and follow the track as it hugs the west side of Claggersnich Wood, following it uphill to the top of the wood. Just as the track begins to descend on the left side, there are a few solitary pine trees and a metal pole indicating the Pipers Stone. The Battle of the Haughs of Cromdale was fought here on 1 May 1690, between Jacobite clans and government troops. The surprise attack of mostly mounted dragoons was more a rout than a battle, ending the Jacobite campaign until the next rising of 1715. Whether true or Victorian romance, a piper playing to encourage his comrades was killed standing by the stone, the Gaelic place name however suggests there was more than one piper.

Follow the track downhill over the site of the battle and make for the road below. Reaching the road, turn left back to Lethendry and Cromdale.

The Pipers Stone

2: Speyside Way and Cromdale Hills

The full length of the right bank of the parish, from Cromdale to Tormore can be walked along the Speyside Way. It follows the old railway line at the start followed by sections, through forestry at Tom an Uird, Knockfrink and Garvault. The Way is well sign posted and is never far from the main road. For the more adventurous, the Cromdale Hills offer great views over Strathspey and Strath Avon. The undulating ridge can be accessed after a steep climb from Bridge of Shennach or near Achvockie Cottage via the track to the transmitter pylon at Tom a'Chait. Carn a Ghille Chear at 710 m (2229 ft) is the highest hill in the parish. Further west along the ridge, Creagan a'Chaise 722 m (2368 ft) with its cairn to commemorate Queen Victoria's Golden Jubilee in 1887, is the highest of the Cromdale Hills, but lies just outside the parish.

3: Advie to Tulchan

The small village of Advie offers a short walk off the A95. Formerly a parish, it comprised the Barony of Advie on the right and Barony of Tulchan on the left banks of the River Spey. It was united with Cromdale in 1593. The church now closed for worship is adjacent to the main road. Built in 1874 it was frequently visited by Edward VII during his hunting, shooting and fishing holidays to Tulchan Lodge. The fragments of a Pictish Class 1 stone found at the site of the original church are built into the vestry wall. Return to the junction and walk down the quieter road passed the hall and the repositioned war memorial, which formerly stood at the apex of the bend. Advie once had its own school, post office and railway station, all of which have now closed. The station was closed in 1965 and had been a busy line serving the numerous distilleries in Speyside. A sign points the way to the cemetery and former site of the original parish church by the banks of the Spey or cross the bridge over the former railway line and continue through the village to Advie Bridge. Opened in 1922 by Mrs McCorquodale of Tulchan Lodge, the concrete single track bridge replaced an earlier wooden one. It over looks Tulchan Pool, one of the many famous salmon pools on this stretch of the Spey.

CHAPTER 8

Rivers and Pools

River Spey

Pools and stretches of the River Spey within Cromdale, Inverallan & Advie Parish. Working downstream from the boundary with Duthil to Knockando and Inveravon parishes

New Spey Bridge

Abernethy Angling Association

1. Tomdhu
2. Upper Railway Pool
3. Lower Railway Pool
4. Croftnahaven
5. Frankie's Corner
6. Nethy Pool
7. Broomhill Pool

Broomhill Bridge

Strathspey Angling Association

8.   Dulnain Mouth Pool
9.   Balliefurth Pool
10. Poll an Eilean
11. Poll Caich
12. Saddle Pool
13. The Bushes Pool
14. Auchernack Burn Pool
15. Little Stream
16. Upper Bend
17. Lower Bend
18. Tarric Mor, Poul Andrew 1808
19. Craggan Sands
20. Poll a Scriodan
21. Poll a Clachan
22. Poll Clach
23. Poll Clachan Lios
24. Finnock Pool
25. Macleod's Pool
26. Poll a Cearan
27. Polnagour

New Spey Bridge

Upper Castle Grant Beat

28. Slop Aindrea

29. Clach na Strone
30. Clach an Uaran
31. Boinne Uaine
32. Big Steam

Old Spey Bridge

33. Bridge Pool
34. Poll na Creice
35. Lurg
36. Bun a Bhord
37. Long Pool
38. Slop Thomas
39. Fail Me Never
40. Upper Slates
41. Lower Slates

Castle Grant

42. Craigroy
43. Uiskano or Eskinore
44. Congash Burn
45. Slop Gachrach or Slodischar
46. Top Sluggan
47. Bottom Sluggan
48. Garrapool or Garra
49. Maggies
50. Bob's Dipper
51. High Church

Cromdale Bridge

52. Bridge Pool or Manse Pool
53. Low Church
54. No1 Burn
55. Back of Island
56. Wash Pot
57. No2 Burn
58. The Cut
59. Croy Race
60. Polcrain
61. Polwick Sluggan
62. Polwick
63. Greenbank
64. Dellifure Pool
65. Bottom Dunbar Sluggan
66. Upper Dunbar
67. Lower Dunbar
68. Dunbar Pool
69. Boundary or March Pool

Tulchan

70. Dolly Pool
71. Gled or Buinne nan Clamhan: Stream or torrent of the buzzards   NJ 0920 3185
72. Bulbain or Dalbain Pool
73. Slopanrone Pool, Dhu or Duple Pool or Poll Dubh: Dark or black pool   NJ 1062 3225   A deep pool situated near the Mains of Dalvey.
74. The Battery

75. Top of Stream or Top of Dalvey, Stream of Dalvey or Buinne Beag: Little cataract   NJ 1106 3224   A narrow part of the River Spey situated a little north of the Mains of Dalvey.

76. Tail of Stream or Tail of Dalvey

77. George Pool

78. Stone Pool

79. Old Woman

80. Broom Pool

81. Poll Crom: Curved or crooked pool   NJ 1189 3334   A deep pool situated a little west of the Croft of Duier.

82. Boat Pool

83. Drain

84. Lodge Stream

85. Rock Pool or Poll na Carriage   Pool of the rook   NJ 1139 3418 A deep salmon pool, situated a little east of Camriach.

86. Spearnack or Speanoch

Advie Bridge

87. Bridge Pool or Tulchan Pool

88. Upper Tulchan

89. Lower Tulchan

90. Dunbar

91. Dummy

92. Straan Pool

93. The Cut

94. Upper Bog

95. Lower Bog

96. Daleigh Stream

97. Daleigh Pool

98. Steading Stream

99. Churchyard Pool or Poll na Ciste: Pool of the chest   NJ 1414 3548 A fishing pool near Dalchroy and north of the old Church of Advie

100. Poll Clach nan Coileach: Pool of the cocks stone   NJ 1443 3568 A fishing pool slightly north of Achvochkie Burn.

101. Stream of Cragganmore

102. Cragganmore or Creagan Mhoir, Head of Wood or Poll a'Chreagain Mhoir: Pool of the large rocky place   NJ 1439 3593 A pool situated opposite a large rock called Creagan Mor.

103. Wood or Poll Dail na Rainich: Pool of the bracken dale or meadow NJ 1445 3614 A fishing pool a little south of the farms of Balnacraobh and Polcreach.

104. Tail of Wood or Poll a' Chreagain Bhig: Pool of the little rocky place   NJ 1487 3648 A deep pool situated about half a mile north west of Fanmore.

105. Hunters

106. Fanmore

107. March Pool or Poll na Cloiche: Pool of the stone NJ 1577 3695 A deep pool partly situated on the boundary between Ballindalloch and Tulchan. Now called the March Pool.

River Dulnain

Pools from confluence with River Spey to boundary with Duthil Parish.

Fly Pool

Railway Pool

Clay Bank

Lochliath

Bridge Pool

Fish Pool

The Falls

The Bulwarks

The Boulders

Long Pool

John's Pool

Castle Benis

The Laundry

Fir Tree

Tommy Rams

Balnaan Pool

Betsy's Pool

Rainbows over Bridge Pool, Pol na Creice

Maps And Plans From The National Records of Scotland

Chapter 1

Register House Plans (RHP)

8921   Plan of the lands of Tullochgorum, Balvattan etc: 1771.

8925   Plan of the farm of Auchnahannet: c.1770.

8926   Plan of the land of Curr: 1771.

8934   Plan of Balnuchk: 19th cent.

13915 Plan of the lands of Clury: 1807.

13924 Plan of Duthil, Tullochgriban and Auchnahannet: 1809.

13935 Plan of the lands of Curr, Clury, Tullochgorum and Gallovie: 1810.

13967 Plan of the lands of Curr, Clury, Tullochgorum and Gallovie: 1810 copied in 1840.

13969 Plan of the lands of Clury: 1807 copied in 1848.

13975 Plan of Duthil, Tullochgriban and Auchnahannet: 1809 copied in 1849.

14019 Plan of Muckrach: 1860.

14023 Plan of the farms of Curr: 1860.

14037 Plan of Auchnahannet: 1860s.

14063 Plan of Balnafoich, Gartenbeg, Toum, Ochnoir, Broompark, Balvattan and Upper Balnacruie: 1860s.

14064 Plan of Torispardon and Croftjames: 1860s.

14070 Plan of Tullochgorum: 1860s.

14072 Plan of farm of Clury: 1860s.

14081 Plan of farms of Coillie na Maoile (Coil-na-Meul), Ruen-Ruich and Rychraggan (Rue Craggan): 1860s.

98222 Sketch plan of 'lines of circumvolation' from Tullochgribban eastward to Auchnahannet: Sept 1767.

98242 Sketch plans of 'lines of circumvolation' from Croftnahaven

(Creitnahaiven) via Tullochgriban to the davoch of Clury: Aug 1767.

98244 Sketch plans of farms of Auchkacoul and Balnaan and part of Clury: Aug 1767.

98245 Sketch plans of mains and subset possessions of the davoch of Clury (Clurie): Aug 1767.

98246 Sketch plans of farm of Wester Curr and Croftnahaven lying along the north side of the Spey: July 1767.

98247 Sketch plan of farm of Tullochgribban and haugh of Clury lying to the south: Aug 1767.

98249 Sketch plans of farm of Easter Curr with the adjoining hill and pasture land and part of Wester Curr lying along the River Spey: July 1767.

98250 Sketch plans of part of the hill and pasture land lying north from Curr: July 1767.

98251 Sketch plan of 'lines of circumvolation' from Tullochgribban to the lime quarry at Muckrach: Aug 1767.

98252 Sketch plans of farm of Auchnahannet and adjoining pasture and moor land: Sept 1767.

98253 Sketch plan of Achna Poet and moor found lying to the south and east: Aug 1767.

98269 Sketch plans of improvements of Coille na Maoile and Ben Ruish with the moor and moss land lying between that an Auchnahannet: Oct 1767.

98276 Sketch plans of improvements of Sleuich and Corseaich: Nov 1767.

98288 Sketch plans of davoch of Tullochgribban: 1767.

98294 Sketch plan of 'lines of circumvolation' from Tullochgorm along the waterside to moor at Gartenbeg and over hills to Duthil: 1767.

Chapter 2

Register House Plans (RHP)

8855 Sketch plan of Inverallan and Craggan: 1770.

8949 Plan of the tacks of Auchnafearn, Ballieward and Lynmacgregor: 1765.

8950 Plan of the lands of Gorton, Auchorsnich and Dreggie: 1767.

8951 Sketch plan of the lands of Grantown-on-Spey (New Grantown) and Kylintra: 1768.

8953 Plan of the Meikle Meadow, Gaich: 1770.

8955 Plan of the farms of Glenbeg, Gorton, Dreggie (Driggie), Kylintra, Drumourachie (Drimuarachie), Craggan and Gaich: 1770.

8957 Plan of Auchnafearn, Tordu, Ballieward, Cottartown and Gaich: c.1770.

8960 Plan of the lands of Glenbeg: 1771.

8961 Plan of the land of Bellintomb [Ballintomb]: 1771.

8973 Plan of the miln croft for the Miln of Craggan: c1800.

8975 Plan of the moor and farms betwixt Ballieward, Carn Luig (Cairnluicht) Wood and Allt an Fhitich (Altnich Burn): 1801.

9026 Portion of plan of the farm of Ballintomb (Bellintomb): 1768.

13911 Plan of Grantown-on-Spey (New Grantown) with the land of Kylintra, Easter and Wester Dreggie etc belonging to James Grant of Grant: 1768.

13928 Plan of the lands of Gorton, Dreggie and Auchnafearn with the village and lands of Grantown-on-Spey, together with Kirktown of Inverallan and Easter Craggan: 1809.

13965 Plan of the lands of Gorton, Dreggie and Auchnafearn with the village and lands of Grantown-on-Spey together with Kirktown of Inverallan and Easter Craggan: 1809 copied in 1844.

98194 Sketch plan of farm of Gorton and moor land between that and Dreggie (Driggy): 1767.

98195 Sketch plan of hilly ground lying north from Auchosnich (Achosnich) and of Creag Beithe (Craigbae): Jul 1767.

98205 1. Sketch plans of farms of Dreggie (Driggy), Auchosnish (Achosnich) and part of Auchnafearn: Jul 1767.

Chapter 3

Register House Plans (RHP)

8855 Sketch plan of Inverallan and Craggan: 1770

8949 Plan of the tacks of Auchnafearn, Ballieward and Lynmacgregor: 1765

8950 Plan of the lands of Gorton, Auchorsnich and Dreggie: 1767

8951 Sketch plan of the lands of Grantown-on-Spey (New Grantown) and Kylintra: 1768

8952 Plan of the farms of West, Upper, Mid and East Port and the moor of Anagach: 1768

8953 Plan of the Meikle Meadow, Gaich: 1770

8955 Plan of the farms of Glenbeg, Gorton, Dreggie (Driggie), Kylintra, Drumourachie (Drimuarachie), Craggan and Gaich: 1770

8956 Plan of Cottartown and Lynmore: c.1770

8957 Plan of Auchnafearn, Tordu, Ballieward, Cottartown and Gaich: c.1770

8958 Plan of part of the grounds about Castle Grant: c.1770

8959 Plan of the lands of Kylintra and Kirktown: 1771

8960 Plan of the lands of Glenbeg: 1771

8961 Plan of the land of Bellintomb [Ballintomb]: 1771

8973 Plan of the miln croft for the Miln of Craggan: c.1800

8974 Plan of the roads betwixt Old Grantown and Castle Grant: c.1800

8975 Plan of the moor and farms betwixt Ballieward, Carn Luig (Cairnluicht) Wood and Allt an Fhitich (Altnich Burn): 1801

8989 Plan of ground betwixt Milton and Heathfield: [early 19th cent]

8992 Plan of the garden of Milton: 1806

9026 Portion of plan of the farm of Ballintomb (Bellintomb): 1768

13911 Plan of Grantown-on-Spey (New Grantown) with the land of Kylintra, Easter and Wester Dreggie etc belonging to James Grant of Grant: 1768

13928 Plan of the lands of Gorton, Dreggie and Auchnafearn with the village and lands of Grantown-on-Spey, together with Kirktown of Inverallan and Easter Craggan: 1809

13965 Plan of the lands of Gorton, Dreggie and Auchnafearn with the village and lands of Grantown-on-Spey together with Kirktown of Inverallan and Easter Craggan: 1809 copied in 1844

81997 Sketch plan of the village of Grantown showing names of occupiers: 1778

98194 Sketch plan of farm of Gorton and moor land between that and Dreggie (Driggy): 1767

98195 Sketch plan of hilly ground lying north from Auchosnich (Achosnich) and of Creag Beithe (Craigbae): Jul 1767

98205 1. Sketch plans of farms of Dreggie (Driggy), Auchosnish (Achosnich) and part of Auchnafearn: Jul 1767

Chapter 4

Register House Plans (RHP)

RHP 8963 Plan of the farms of Culfoichmore, Upper Delliefure, Lower Delliefure: 1780.

RHP 8982 Plan of the farms of Auchnahannet (Achnahannet, Auchnagallin (Achnagaul), Ballinlagg (Bellenluig) and Knockannakeist: 1802.

RHP 8985 Plan of Tombain, Uchtugorm, Auchnarrowbeg and Craigbeg: c.1802.

RHP 13930 Plan of Auchnarrowmore, Auchnarrowbeg and Lynmore: 1810.

RHP 13931 Plan of Auchnagallin and Auchnahannet: 1810.

RHP 13949 Plan of the lands of Miltown and Ports: 1771

RHP 13959 Plan of Auchnarrowmore, Auchnarrowbeg and Lynmore: 1810, copied in 1843.

RHP 13960 Plan of Auchnagallin and Auchnahannet: 1810 copied in 1849.

RHP 98230 Sketch plans of improvements of Knock Auchnahannet and Lyntaurie (Meikle and Little Lensouries): Jul 1767.

RHP 98231 Sketch plans of farms of Wester Auchnagallin (Auchnygaull) and part of the moss and moor lying to south west: July 1767.

RHP 98234 Sketch plans of farms of Auchnarrowmore, Balnaclash and Culquhourn: July 1767.

RHP 98235 Sketch plan of part of farms of Easter and Wester Delliefure lying along River Spey: July 1767.

RHP 98236 Sketch plans of 'lines of circumvolation' from moss at Balnaclash to Cottartown and round by Park of Dellyfure: June 1767.

RHP 98291 Sketch plans of Derraid (Dirryrait) and the hill and moor lying north from Lynmore (Linemore): 1767.

RHP 98293 Sketch plans of davoch and hill of Auchnarrowmore: July 1767.

RHP 98399 Sketch plans of farms of Easter Auchnagallin (Auchnagaul), Knock of Auchnahannet and part of Auchnahannet (Achnyhannet): July 1767.

Chapter 5

Register House Plans (RHP)

RHP 8954 Plan of the farm of Knockanbuie: c.1770.

RHP 8979 Plan of Wester and Easter Lettoch, Wester Culfoich, Culfoichbeg and Laglia: 1802.

RHP 13951 Plan of the davoch of Skiradvy (Advie), Morayshire: 1804.

RHP 13952 Plan of the lands of Tulchan: 1804.

RHP 13955 Plan of the lands of Tulchan: 1804, copied in 1842.

RHP 13956 Plan of the davoch of Advie (Skiradvie): 1804, copied in 1842.

RHP 98211 Sketch plans of Easter and Wester Lettoch and Culfoichbeg (Culquoichbegg): c.1767.

RHP 98237 Sketch plan of improvements called Lettoch (Derry Lettoch): June 1767.

Chapter 6

Register House Plans (RHP)

9005 Plan of Lochindorb: [post 1809].

13922 Plan of the hills lying south of Lochindorb, including the improvements of Crannich, Ryneckra (Ruenechkera) and Glentarroch (Glen Tearroch):1809.

13958 Plan of the hills lying south of Lochindorb, including the improvements of Crannich, Rynechkra (Ruenechkera) and Glentarroch (Glen Tearroch): 1809, copied in 1848.

13961 Plan of the improvement of Ourack (Aurack) and adjoining hill pasture: 1812, copied in 1846.

13962 Plan of Dava, Ruigh Thuim (Rue Huin), Badahad (Badagat) etc: 1810, copied in 1845.

13958 Plan of the hills lying south of Lochindorb, including the improvements of Crannich, Rynechkra (Ruenechkera) and Glentarroch (Glen Tearroch): 1809, copied in 1848

Chapter 7

Register House Plans (RHP)

RHP 8863 Plan of road from the Bridge of Avon to Dalvey: 1811.

RHP 8966 Plan of lands between the Milton and Mains of Dalvey, Morayshire: c.1790.

RHP 8968 Plan of the farm of Airdbeg: 18th cent.

RHP 8972 Plan of the farms of Easter and Wester Rynabeallich: c.1800.

RHP 13914 Plan of the davoch of Dalvey: 1804 (Vignette of cherub etc):1804.

RHP 13929 Plan of the davoch of Dalchapple (Dellachapple): c.1809.

RHP 13951 Plan of the davoch of Skiradvy [Advie]:1804.

RHP 13952 Plan of the lands of Tulchan: 1804.

RHP 13955 Plan of the lands of Tulchan: 1804 copied in 1842.

RHP 13956 Plan of the davoch of Advie (Skiradvy):1804 copied in 1842.

RHP 13990 Plan of Strathspey from Grantown-on-Spey to Ballindalloch: 1862-1865.

RHP 14076 Plan of Pollowick, Dalchapple (Dellachaple) and part of Tom an Uird (Touminourd): 1860.

RHP 14077 Plan of Balmenach and Burnside: 1860s.

RHP 14078 Plan of farm of Dalvey: 1862.

RHP 14079 Plan of Garvault, Airdbeg and Mains of Advie: 1860.

RHP 98192   1.Sketch plan of the davoch of Lethendry called Ballachule with part of Easter and Wester Lethendry: May 1767.

                2. Notes of names of farms in the davochs of Dalchapple, Lethendry and Burnside: 1767.

RHP 98202 Sketch plans of farm of Rynnabealich from the march of Wester Shennach to cornlands of Tominourd and of improvable land called Allanmore: May 1767.

RHP 98203 Sketch plans of 'lines of circumvolation' of farms of Rynnabealich and the Lethendrys, part of Burnside and the hill of Tominourd, annotated: May 1767.

RHP 98204 Sketch plan of farm of Auldcharn (Altacharn): May 1767.

RHP 98209 Sketch plans of 'lines of circumvolation' from River Spey at Cromdale via Speybridge and Auldcharn (Altcharn) to Burnside: c.1767.

RHO 98212 Plans, with wrapper, of part of Ballachule (Bellychule) and Lethendry and the improvements beside River Spey, Morayshire: 1767.

RHP 98212/1 Plans of part of Ballachule (Bellychule) and Lethendry and improvements beside the River Spey between Dalvey and Cromdale, Morayshire May: 1767.

RHP 98212/2 Bundle wrapper to sketch plans of lands in the parish of Cromdale and on south side of River Spey, Morayshire: May 1767.

RHP 98214 Sketch plans of farm of Burnside, Tomlea and part of Balmenach, and part of Easter and Wester Lethendry lying along the march of Balmenach, Cullinduim, Croftindam and Miln Croft: May 1767.

RHP 98215 Sketch plans of 'lines of circumvolation' from the hill of Tomlea via Lethendry westward to Burnside with lines of intersections to the neighbouring hills: c. 1767.

RHP 98263 Sketch plans of Dalvey: c.1767.

RHP 98265 Sketch plans of part of miln croft and improvements of Bruntland: May 1767.

RHP 98297 Sketch plans of farms of Tominourd, Balnafettach, Tomnagaun, Dalchapple and Pollowick: May 1767.

RHP 98298 Plans of parts of Easter and Wester Lethendry, Cullinduim, Croftindam and Milton of Cromdale lying along the march of Balmenach, Morayshire: May 1767.

RHP 98299 Sketch plans of davoch of Dalvey containing part of the Mains of Shanvell 'with the lines of survey and the intersections of the hills (plan no1 of Dalvey): May 1767.

RHP 98300 Sketch plans of davoch of Dalvey containing the farms of Aird, Easter and Wester Shennach and Balnallan (plan no 2 of Dalvey): May 1767.

RHP 98301 Plans of part of Mains of Dalvey, Milton, Knockailsch and Achenearnach, with notes and observations on divisions, farming and tenants of davoch of Dalvey, Morayshire: May 1767.

RHP 98302 Sketch plans of farm of Advie: 2 Feb 1770.

RHP 98369 Sketch plans of lands of Advie: c. 1770.

Bibliography

Cromdale, Inverallan and Advie Census Returns 1841-1911

Cromdale, Inverallan and Advie Old Parish Register CH2/128B/1 et seq

Cromdale Parish Kirk Session Records CH2/983/1 et seq

Cromdale, Inverallan and Advie Parish Valuation Rolls

Drummond, P. (1991) Scottish Hill and Mountaineering Names (Scottish Mountaineering Trust)

Dwelly, E. (1994) The Illustrated Gaelic- English Dictionary, Gairm, Inverness

Farrell, S. (2011) Monumental Inscriptions Cromdale Churchyard, Badenoch & Strathspey, Highland Family History Society, Inverness

Forsyth, Rev. Dr W. (1900) In the Shadow of Cairngorm. Inverness

Matheson, D (1905) The Place Names of Elginshire, Stirling

MacGregor, N. (1995). Gaelic place-names in Strathspey. Transactions of the Gaelic Society of Inverness 58, 299-370

MacGregor, N. (1997). Gaelic in Strathspey. Transactions of the Gaelic Society of Inverness 59, 488-606

Mitchell, A. (1974) Pre-1855 Gravestone Inscriptions on Speyside, The Scottish Genealogical Society. Edinburgh.

Murray J. (2014) Reading The Gaelic Landscape Whittles Publishing Ltd, Dunbeath.

New Statistical Account, Vol. 14, Cromdale Parish. Rev James Grant

Old Statistical Account Rev Lewis Grant Cromdale

Nicolaisen W.F.H. (1976) Scottish Place-Names London

Nicolaisen W.F.H. The distribution of certain Gaelic Mountain Names Transactions of the Gaelic Society of Inverness 45 (1969) 113-128.

Ordnance Survey Name Book for Cromdale and Inverallan RH/4/23/142

Ordnance Survey 6" to a mile map of Grantown 1st ed surveyed 1869-71 pub 1873.

Ordnance Survey 1:25000 Explorer Map 418 Lochindorb, Grantown on Spey and Carrbridge

Ordnance Survey 1:25000 Explorer Map 419 Grantown on Spey and Hills of Cromdale

Pont, T 1590s National Library of Scotland Pont Maps

Rennie J.A. (1951) In The Steps of The Clansmen, Rich & Cowan, London

Rennie J.A. (1956) Romantic Strathspey, Its Lands, Clans and Legends R. Hale, London

Roy Military Maps 1746-55

Sinclair J. (ed) (1791-99) The Statistical Account of Scotland, Edinburgh.

Smith C.M (1957) Strathspey Highways and Byways, Moray & Nairn Newspaper Co Ltd, Elgin

Strathspey Herald Newspaper Jan 22 1932 and Jan 29 1932. 'Place Names Around Grantown'.

Stuart, A Place Names of Strathspey by a native, reprinted from 'The Strathspey News'.

Watson, A. (2013). Place names in much of north-east Scotland. Paragon Publishing, Rothersthorpe.

Watson, W.J. (1993) The Celtic Placenames of Scotland, Edinburgh.

Lightning Source UK Ltd.
Milton Keynes UK
UKHW020635050419
340474UK00007B/60/P